100 AMAZING FACTS ABOUT GREEK MYTHOLOGY

© 2023, Marc Dresgui

Content

Introduction 8

Fact 1 - Zeus, the king who controls lightning bolts 9

Fact 2 - Persephone, Queen of the Underworld part-time 10

Fact 3 - The Nemean Lion Only Hercules Could Defeat 11

Fact 4 - Medusa turns anyone who looks at her to stone 12

Fact 5 - The Unstoppable Shield of Achilles 13

Fact 6 - The Tragic Wax Wings of Icarus 14

Fact 7 - Narcissus, the lover of his reflection 15

Fact 8 - Apollo drives the chariot of the sun every day 16

Fact 9 - Pegasus, the winged horse born of a monster 17

Fact 10 - Poseidon and his horses galloping on the water 18

Fact 11 - Pandora and the Box of Woes 19

Fact 12 - Athena is born from the head of Zeus 20

Fact 13 - The Sirens Who Sing to Trap Sailors 21

Fact 14 - Dionysus, god of wine and feasting 22

Fact 15 - Odysseus' tricks in the face of the Cyclops 23

Fact 16 - The Surprise in the Trojan Horse 24

Fact 17 - Atlas, doomed to carry the sky 25

Fact 18 - Echo, the nymph who can only repeat 26

Fact 19 - Breadcrumbs' thread to get out of the labyrinth 27

Fact 20 - Hermès, the messenger with wings on his feet 28

Fact 21 - Hephaestus, the lame blacksmith of the gods 29

Fact 22 - The Golden Apples That Cause Quarrels 30

Fact 23 - Orpheus' Journey to the Underworld for Eurydice.........31

Fact 24 - Arachnea Woven into a Spider by Athena....................32

Fact 25 - The Forbidden Love of Psyche and Eros........................33

Fact 26 - Demeter's Revenge and Famine......................................34

Fact 27 - Pygmalion falls in love with a statue..............................35

Fact 28 - Prometheus, the Fire Thief for Humans.......................36

Fact 29 - Apollo's Lyre That Charms Everyone.............................37

Fact 30 - The Hyades, Nymphs Transformed into Stars.............38

Fact 31 - Hermès' winged sandals..39

Fact 32 - The War Between Athena and Poseidon for Athens.....40

Fact 33 - Chimeras, Beasts with Many Faces................................41

Fact 34 - The Atalanta Race and the Golden Apples...................42

Fact 35 - Aphrodite, born from the foam of the sea...................43

Fact 36 - Theseus fights the Minotaur..44

Fact 37 - Orpheus' Magic Harp...45

Fact 38 - The Moires Who Spin Destiny...46

Fact 39 - Midas and Everything He Touches Turns Gold.............47

Fact 40 - Medea's Revenge on Jason..48

Fact 41 - The Sharp Claws of the Sphinx.......................................49

Fact 42 - The Maden Dance..50

Fact 43 - Hades' Invisibility Helmet...51

Fact 44 - The Fall of Icarus Too Close to the Sun........................52

Fact 45 - Calydon's Gigantic Boar Hunt...53

Fact 46 - The Nereids, Nymphs of the Seas..................................54

Fact 47 - Poseidon's trident that makes the earth shake 55

Fact 48 - The Dreams Sent by Morpheus 56

Fact 49 - The Heavy Weight of Sisyphus to Roll Forever 57

Fact 50 - Zeus' tricks to seduce 58

Fact 51 - The Fury of Hera, Jealous of Zeus' Love 59

Fact 52 - The Gorgoneion, Athena's Fearsome Shield 60

Fact 53 - The Twelve Labors Imposed on Hercules 61

Fact 54 - The Mysterious Oracle of Delphi 62

Fact 55 - Niobe's Revenge Turned into a Rock 63

Fact 56 - Hundred-eyed Argos watches over Io 64

Fact 57 - Penelope's Magic Tapestry 65

Fact 58 - The Argonauts in Search of the Golden Fleece 66

Fact 59 - Tithon's Fountain of Youth 67

Fact 60 - The Unleashed Breath of the Aeolus Winds 68

Fact 61 - Hermes' tricks to deceive Argos 69

Fact 62 - The Northern Lights, Aurora Dances 70

Fact 63 - Samson's strength, given by Zeus 71

Fact 64 - The Secrets of Mount Olympus 72

Fact 65 - The Musical Challenge Between Pan and Apollo 73

Fact 66 - The Wrath of Zeus Turns Lycaon into a Wolf 74

Fact 67 - The Incredible Adventures of Perseus 75

Fact 68 - Aphrodite's Beauty Bath 76

Fact 69 - The Punishment of Thirsty Tantalus 77

Fact 70 - Andromeda's prowess against a monster 78

Fact 71 - Athena's Protection of the City of Athens 79
Fact 72 - The Healing Power of the Centaur Chiron 80
Fact 73 - The Lotus Flower Trap for Odysseus 81
Fact 74 - The misadventures of Io, pursued by a horsefly 82
Fact 75 - The Abduction of Europa by Zeus in Bull 83
Fact 76 - Hephaestus' Laughter That Makes Olympus Tremble . 84
Fact 77 - The Golden Rain, Zeus' gift to Danaë 85
Fact 78 - Ganymede's Rise to the Rank of Deity 86
Fact 79 - Aphrodite's Magic Mirror 87
Fact 80 - Aurora's Tears Turning Dew 88
Fact 81 - Apples of Discord, Cause of Great Quarrels 89
Fact 82 - Achilles' Journey to the Realm of the Dead 90
Fact 83 - Apollo's Laurel Wreath 91
Fact 84 - The Sweet Sleep Induced by Hypnos 92
Fact 85 - The Power of the Muses on Inspiration 93
Fact 86 - The Sacred Fire Guarded by the Vestal Virgins 94
Fact 87 - The Birth of Dionysus from a Thigh of Zeus 95
Fact 88 - The Dance of the Stars, Girls of Atlas 96
Fact 89 - The Sun's Course, Drawn by Helios 97
Fact 90 - The Story of Cephalus and the Dawn 98
Fact 91 - The Adventures of Odysseus and the Sirens 99
Fact 92 - The Beauty of Adonis Who Seduces Two Goddesses 100
Fact 93 - The Snake Charmer Asclepius 101
Fact 94 - The Exploits of the Hero Bellerophon 102

Fact 95 - The Eternal Wisdom of Athena's Owl 103

Fact 96 - The Tragic Love of Eros and Psyche 104

Fact 97 - The Island of the Lotus Eaters 105

Fact 98 - Niobe's Weeping Becomes an Eternal Source 106

Fact 99 - Theseus' Victory over Procrustes 107

Fact 100 - The Morning Star, Symbol of Hope 108

Conclusion 109

Quiz 110

Answers 116

"Greek mythology is not only a religious narrative of the past, but also an eternal inspiration for our daily lives."

— *Carl Jung*

Introduction

Welcome, dear reader, to the fascinating world of Greek mythology, a world full of mysteries, heroes, gods and extraordinary creatures. Through these pages, you are invited to dive into the heart of an ancient culture that has shaped history and continues to influence our world today. "100 Amazing Facts About Greek Mythology" is designed to guide you on an epic journey, revealing stories and secrets that have survived the test of time.

Each fact presented here is a window into the myths and legends that have captured the imagination of generations. You'll discover wayward gods, valiant heroes, perilous quests, and immortal loves. These stories, filled with wisdom, bravery and passion, are much more than just stories; They reflect the hopes, dreams and fears of an entire civilization.

So, open your eyes wide and prepare to be amazed, because Greek mythology is an inexhaustible treasure trove of wonders and discoveries. Happy reading!

Marc Dresgui

Fact 1 - Zeus, the king who controls lightning bolts

Hail there, young adventurer of knowledge! Have you ever heard of Zeus, the all-powerful god of Mount Olympus? He's the king of the gods in Greek mythology, and he has a really impressive special ability: he can control lightning!

Just imagine! When Zeus is angry or wants to show his power, he shoots lightning bolts from the sky. These lightning bolts are like his personal javelins. For example, he once used this power to punish certain mortals or other gods who had defied him. It's a bit like having a giant remote control to control the weather, but much more spectacular!

But Zeus is not just an angry god. These lightning bolts also symbolize his justice and authority over the world. So, the next time you hear thunder rumble or see lightning streaking across the sky, think of Zeus and the incredible power he holds!

And don't forget, mythology is full of these fantastic stories. Are you ready to discover more?

Fact 2 - Persephone, Queen of the Underworld part-time

Hey, curious about the mythological world! Have you ever heard the intriguing story of Persephone? She is the daughter of Demeter, the goddess of harvests, and has an unusual life, to say the least. Indeed, she is queen of the Underworld... but only half the time!

One day, while she was picking flowers, Hades, the god of the Underworld, kidnapped her and took her to his underground realm. Impressive, isn't it? Despite this terrifying situation, she has become the queen of this dark world. But his story doesn't end there. Thanks to a special agreement, she spends six months in the Underworld and the other six months on Earth with her mother.

This double life has a direct consequence on our planet. When Persephone is in the Underworld, her mother Demeter is so sad that she brings winter to Earth. But when Persephone returns, it's spring! Nature is reborn, flowers are blooming, and everything is celebrating.

It's fascinating to think that the changing of the seasons, which we observe every year, is linked to the story of a goddess who lives between two worlds. What do you think?

Fact 3 - The Nemean Lion Only Hercules Could Defeat

Hello, future expert in ancient myths! Are you ready to hear about the Nemean lion, a creature so ferocious that no one could defeat it... except for a certain hero named Hercules? Hold on tight, because this story is full of action and bravery!

The Nemean lion was no ordinary lion. His skin was so strong that weapons could not pierce it. Imagine an invincible animal, terrifying anyone who dared to approach its territory. Defeating this monster was one of the twelve tasks that Hercules had to complete.

But how could you defeat a beast that could not be hurt by swords and arrows? Hercules, with his strength and intelligence, decided to fight the lion with his bare hands. After a fierce struggle, he managed to strangle the lion, proving his bravery.

This story shows not only Hercules' incredible strength, but also his courage and determination. It reminds us that with perseverance, we can overcome any challenge. Feeling inspired?

Fact 4 - Medusa turns anyone who looks at her to stone

Hey, young explorer of legends! Have you ever met a person whose gaze was so intense that it froze you in place? This is exactly what happened with Medusa, one of the three Gorgons, but with an even more terrifying effect: she turned anyone who met her eyes to stone!

Medusa wasn't always a scary creature. She was once a beautiful priestess, but as a result of a tragic event, she was cursed and her beautiful hair turned into poisonous snakes. No wonder she scares so many people with such an appearance!

But his power was not invincible. A hero named Perseus took up the challenge of decapitating her without ever meeting her eyes. Using a reflective shield given to him by Athena, he used Medusa's reflection to locate and shoot her.

This story of Medusa shows us that no matter the strength or curse, there is always a solution or weakness to exploit. So, are you ready to discover more secrets of mythology?

Fact 5 - The Unstoppable Shield of Achilles

Hello, passionate about ancient heroes! Have you ever dreamed of having a magic shield to protect you from any danger? Well, Achilles, the greatest warrior of the Trojan War, had exactly that: a special shield designed by Hephaestus, the blacksmith god.

This shield was no ordinary one. It was incredibly resilient and adorned with wonderful images depicting the sky, the sea, battles and even parties! Every detail engraved on it told a story, making this shield not only a protection, but also a true work of art.

With this shield in hand, Achilles was virtually invincible in battle. He wore it proudly in battle, and it inspired both fear and admiration in his enemies. But remember, even with such an object, Achilles had a weak point: his heel.

This history teaches us that no matter how strong or protective we are, we all have vulnerabilities. And you, if you had a magic shield, what would it look like?

Fact 6 - The Tragic Wax Wings of Icarus

Hail, Adventurer of Distant Legends! Have you ever dreamed of flying like a bird, free in the blue sky? Icarus, a young boy from Greek mythology, was so lucky... but with unintended consequences.

His father, Daedalus, was a brilliant inventor. To escape a labyrinth on the island of Crete, he designed wings for himself and his son, made from feathers and fixed with wax. Thanks to them, they would be able to fly away and regain their freedom.

Icarus was amazed by the sensation of flying. But, carried away by euphoria, he disobeyed his father's advice and flew too close to the sun. The heat melted the wax, and the feathers came off. Unfortunately, Icarus fell into the sea and drowned.

This sad story reminds us of the importance of listening and being careful. Dreams can come true, but you also need to know your limits. And you, how far would you go to make your dreams come true?

Fact 7 - Narcissus, the lover of his reflection

Hello, curious about the fascinating stories of yesteryear! Have you ever heard of Narcissus? No, not the flower, but a young man from Greek mythology, known for his beauty... and for his obsessive love of himself.

Narcissus was so handsome that everyone who crossed his path fell in love with him. But he repulsed everybody, convinced that no love could equal his own beauty. One day, near a spring of clear water, he saw his reflection and fell madly in love... of itself!

He spent days and nights gazing at his image in the water, unable to detach himself from it. He forgot to eat, to drink, and finally succumbed to sadness and despair, transforming into the flower we now call the narcissus.

This legend shows us the importance of humility and the dangers of obsession. Loving and respecting yourself is great, but loving yourself too much can drive you away from others. And you, what do you think of this story? Do you think balance is key?

Fact 8 - Apollo drives the chariot of the sun every day

Hail to you, lover of celestial mysteries! Did you know that every time the sun rises, it's actually a god who takes the reins of a magnificent chariot? Let me introduce you to Apollo, the Greek god of the sun, music and poetry.

In ancient Greece, it was imagined that the sun was a luminous chariot pulled by powerful horses. And who else but Apollo, with his strength and charisma, could lead such a team across the sky? Every morning it soared from the east, illuminating the world with its golden rays.

But driving this tank was not easy. The horses were fiery and fiery, and perfect control was required to steer them over the celestial vault, thus ensuring the smooth course of the sun.

This myth illustrates the importance of consistency and dedication. Apollo, with his daily task, reminds us that every day is a new opportunity, a new journey to undertake. So, are you ready to seize the day in the manner of Apollo?

Fact 9 - Pegasus, the winged horse born of a monster

Hey, explorer of amazing myths! Have you ever dreamed of riding a horse that could fly? That's exactly what Pegasus, the famous winged horse, was. But do you know where it comes from?

Pegasus was not born like other horses. It appeared incredibly, gushing from Medusa's blood when she was defeated by the hero Perseus. Unbelievable, right? From a heroic act was born this magnificent horse with large white wings.

During his lifetime, Pegasus accomplished many feats. One of the most famous is when he helped another hero, Bellerophon, defeat the terrifying Chimera. Together, they flew high in the sky, fighting monsters and performing feats.

The legend of Pegasus shows us that beauty and grandeur can arise from the most unexpected places. It is the symbol of inspiration and aspiration to reach new heights. And you, would you like to have a companion as loyal and majestic as Pegasus for your adventures?

Fact 10 - Poseidon and his horses galloping on the water

Hello, adventurer of the mysterious seas! Have you ever seen a horse galloping on water? No? So, let me tell you about Poseidon, the mighty god of the sea, and his incredible water horses.

Poseidon, with his fearsome trident, ruled all the oceans and seas of the Earth. But that wasn't its only peculiarity. He had special horses, with the unique ability to gallop over the waves as if it were a green meadow.

These horses were his pride. Majestic and powerful, they could unleash storms or calm raging seas. When Poseidon rode his chariot pulled by them, even the sea creatures stopped to admire this impressive sight.

The story of Poseidon and his horses teaches us respect for the forces of nature and the beauty that lies in mastered power. Imagine the feeling of galloping on the waves, hair blowing in the wind, alongside the great god of the sea! Fascinating, isn't it?

Fact 11 - Pandora and the Box of Woes

Hello, curious about ancient mysteries! Have you ever heard the expression "open Pandora's box"? Here's the fascinating story behind that phrase.

Pandora, created by the gods, was given a mysterious box as a gift with a strict instruction: never open it. But sometimes curiosity is stronger than anything, isn't it? Well, Pandora couldn't resist the temptation and lifted the lid.

When she opened the box, all the ills of the world escaped: sadness, illness, anger... Only hope, small and frail, remained in the background, like a ray of light in the darkness.

This story is a reminder of how curiosity is both a blessing and a source of danger. It also teaches us that after dark times, there is always a glimmer of hope. What do you think? Would you have resisted the urge to open this mysterious box?

Fact 12 - Athena is born from the head of Zeus

Hello, friend of amazing stories! Would it have ever occurred to you that a god could be born... a head? Unbelievable, isn't it? And yet, this is how Athena was born.

Zeus, the king of the gods, had a terrible headache. It wasn't just a headache like you might have, but something gigantic, cosmic! By the way, this headache was not due to chance.

With the help of Hephaestus, god of fire and forge, his skull was cut open. And to everyone's surprise, Athena emerged, already an adult, dressed in her shining armor, ready to fight and defend wisdom and justice.

This unique mode of birth reflects the power and wisdom of Athena, one of the most revered goddesses of ancient Greece. And you, what do you think of this spectacular birth? Not like the others, huh?

Fact 13 - The Sirens Who Sing to Trap Sailors

Hey, maritime adventure lover! Have you ever heard of half-woman, half-bird creatures that sang so beautifully that sailors couldn't resist? This is the story of the mermaids of Greek mythology.

In the deep and mysterious waters of ancient Greece, lived mermaids, beings with bewitching voices. When they sang, their melody was so irresistible that sailors were drawn to them, forgetting everything around them.

But be careful! These songs were not innocent. Mermaids used their voices to lure sailors to sharp rocks, causing their ships to sink. It was a death trap from which few could escape.

Odysseus, the hero of the famous story "The Odyssey", knew how to avoid their charm. He had his sailors' ears plugged with wax and had himself tied to the mast of his ship so that he could hear their song safely. Clever, isn't it? Do you think you could have resisted their haunting singing?

Fact 14 - Dionysus, god of wine and feasting

Hello, lover of good stories and celebrations! Do you know Dionysus, the god who knew how to party? Here's what you need to know about him.

Dionysus is the son of Zeus, the king of the gods, and a mortal woman. He was not only the god of wine, but also of feasts, theatre and ecstasy. Imagine a god who embodies joy, dance and music, it was him!

With a glass of wine always in hand, Dionysus traveled around the world teaching humans the art of viticulture. Thanks to him, humans learned how to cultivate vines and produce wine. You can thank him for all the joyful festivities!

But Dionysus wasn't just associated with joy. There was also a dark side to him. Those who opposed him or his teachings could meet his wrath. So, the next time you raise your glass of grape juice, think of Dionysus and his incredible legacy!

Fact 15 - Odysseus' tricks in the face of the Cyclops

Hey, you who love stories of adventure and cunning! Have you ever heard of the encounter between Odysseus and the terrifying Cyclops? Hold on tight, because it's a thrilling story!

During his travels, Odysseus and his crew find themselves on an island, and they decide to explore a large cave. Surprise! They come face to face with a giant cyclops named Polyphemus. This monster, with a large eye in the middle of its forehead, locks Odysseus and his companions in the cave to eat them one by one.

Odysseus, always clever, hatches a plan. He introduces himself to the Cyclops as "Nobody". After intoxicating the Cyclops with wine, Odysseus and his men drive a sharp stake into his single eye, blinding him. When the other Cyclops rush to help Polyphemus, he yells at them that "Nobody" is attacking him, leaving them perplexed.

The ruse doesn't stop there! To escape from the cave, Odysseus and his men hide under Polyphemus' sheep. The Cyclops, no longer able to see, suspects nothing when the heroes escape safely. Thanks to his intelligence, Odysseus once again shows why he is one of the most famous heroes in mythology!

Fact 16 - The Surprise in the Trojan Horse

Ah, the famous Trojan horse! If you're curious, you've probably heard this term, but do you really know the story behind it? Let's dive into one of the greatest stratagems in Greek mythology.

After years of unsuccessful siege before the walls of Troy, the Greeks seem to have given up. They leave behind a huge wooden horse as an offering to the gods. The Trojans, thinking it was a sign of victory, dragged the horse inside their walls. Big mistake!

What the Trojans don't know is that the horse is not just a statue. Inside, lurking Greek soldiers led by Odysseus, ready to strike at the most unexpected moment. When night falls, they get out of the horse and open the gates of the city, allowing the Greek army to enter and conquer Troy.

This trick, this trick of war, has become so famous that today the "Trojan horse" has become synonymous with hidden deception or surprise. A memorable lesson on the importance of always being wary of appearances!

Fact 17 - Atlas, doomed to carry the sky

You've probably seen statues or depictions of a muscular man carrying the world on his shoulders, haven't you? That man is Atlas, a titan from Greek mythology. But do you really know why he's carrying this burden?

The story begins with the Titanomachy, a titanic war between the Titans and the gods of Olympus. Atlas, being on the side of the Titans, played a crucial role in this battle. However, as is often the case in wars, there are winners and losers. Unfortunately for Atlas, the Titans lost.

As punishment for rebelling against the Olympians, Zeus condemned Atlas to carry the sky on his shoulders for eternity. Yes, you heard that right, eternity! He had to make sure that heaven and earth would never meet.

Whenever you hear about Atlas or see a depiction of him, remember this fascinating story. It is a powerful symbol of the weight of the consequences of our actions and the fate from which there is no escape.

Fact 18 - Echo, the nymph who can only repeat

In the vast and captivating world of Greek mythology, the story of Echo stands out for its melancholy and tragic romanticism. Echo was a talkative nymph with a melodious voice and an unparalleled talent for conversation. She had, however, an unfortunate tendency to distract Hera, the wife of Zeus, with her long speeches, thus allowing Zeus' love affairs to slip unnoticed.

Angered by these shenanigans, Hera decided to punish Echo by depriving her of her voice, leaving her with the ability to repeat the last words spoken by others. This curse, far from being insignificant, was to change the nymph's destiny forever.

When Echo crossed paths with Narcissus, a breathtakingly beautiful young man, she fell head over heels in love with him. But unable to declare her love for him, she could only repeat the last words of his sentences. Unaware of the curse, Narcissus cruelly repulsed it.

Heartbroken, Echo allowed herself to be consumed by her unrequited love, slowly turning to stone, leaving behind only her ethereal voice. His story, imbued with sadness, continues to resonate like an echo through the ages, reminding us of the sometimes tragic consequences of unrequited love.

Fact 19 - Breadcrumbs' thread to get out of the labyrinth

In the intricate interweaving of Greek mythology, the story of Ariadne's thread occupies a prominent place, a wonderful illustration of human ingenuity in the face of adversity. Ariadne, daughter of King Minos of Crete, fell madly in love with Theseus, who had come from Athens to try to defeat the Minotaur, a half-man, half-bull creature locked in a labyrinth.

Aware of the almost unsolvable complexity of the labyrinth designed by Daedalus, Ariadne decided to help Theseus by offering him a red thread, allowing him to retrace his path once the Minotaur was defeated. It was a bold move, filled with both love and rebellion against his own father.

With the help of this thread, Theseus not only managed to kill the Minotaur, but also to escape the labyrinth, a feat that had previously seemed impossible. He took Ariadne with him on his ship, but later abandoned her on the island of Naxos, an act whose reasons remain unclear and subject to interpretation.

The story of Ariadne's thread has been remembered as a symbol of love, betrayal and ingenuity, proving once again the richness and complexity of Greek myths. It teaches us that even in the most desperate situations, a thread of hope can always guide us to the exit.

Fact 20 - Hermès, the messenger with wings on his feet

If you've ever seen an image of a winged god, wearing a hat and sandals adorned with wings, chances are you've crossed paths with Hermes, the messenger of the gods in Greek mythology. Son of Zeus and Maia, Hermes was known for his speed and agility, symbolized by the wings attached to his feet and hat, the petase.

Hermes was not only the messenger of the gods, he was also the protector of travelers, thieves, and traders. He had the ability to move freely between the mortal world and the world of the gods, a valuable skill that allowed him to convey divine messages to humans. Among his most famous exploits, he helped Zeus fight the Titans and saved Greek heroes from perilous situations several times.

This easy-spoken and mischievous god also had a gift for negotiation and mediation, often acting as a peacemaker between the gods. Its attributes, such as the caduceus, a staff surrounded by two serpents, became symbols of communication and trade.

The history of Hermès teaches us the importance of communication and diplomacy, and its legacy lives on to the present day, with its name even used to describe a style of fast delivery: express shipping. So, the next time you see a package coming in at full speed, remember Hermes, the divine messenger who never failed to deliver on time.

Fact 21 - Hephaestus, the lame blacksmith of the gods

Among the pantheon of Greek deities, Hephaestus stands out for his unparalleled talent in the art of forging and his limping gait. Son of Zeus and Hera, he was born lame, which caused him to be rejected by his mother who threw him from the top of Olympus. This fall did not dampen his creative and ingenious spirit, and Hephaestus became the official blacksmith of the gods, crafting weapons and jewelry of unparalleled beauty and power.

His workshop was in the burning bowels of Mount Etna, where he created, among other things, the thunderbolts of Zeus, the armor of Achilles, and the shield of Heracles. Despite his disability, Hephaestus mastered fire and metals like no other, and his creations were always imbued with perfection.

His love life was just as tumultuous, married to Aphrodite, the goddess of love and beauty, and he had to put up with her infidelities. But Hephaestus did not let himself be discouraged and used his ingenuity to take his revenge, illustrating his cunning and skill.

Hephaestus teaches us that despite obstacles and rejections, perseverance and talent can lead to excellence and recognition. His legacy lives on in the history of art and metallurgy, making him an eternal example of resilience and creativity.

Fact 22 - The Golden Apples That Cause Quarrels

In Greek mythology, the golden apples in the garden of the Hesperides were a source of lust and conflict. These precious fruits were guarded by nymphs at the western end of the known world, and their brilliance and value were immeasurable. They were so coveted that even the gods couldn't resist the urge to possess them, causing disputes and feuds.

Perhaps the most famous of these apples is the one that Paris, prince of Troy, gave to Aphrodite, choosing beauty and love over wisdom and power. This gesture was the spark that ignited the Trojan War, a devastating conflict that marked Greek mythological history.

The works of Heracles, another epic tale, included the near-impossible task of picking these golden apples. Heracles, with cunning and force, finally managed to seize the fruits, demonstrating that even the most precious and guarded possessions are not out of reach.

These stories remind us that lust can lead to major conflicts, and that high-value items can be both a blessing and a curse. Golden apples remain a powerful symbol of the unintended consequences that our desires can have on our destiny.

Fact 23 - Orpheus' Journey to the Underworld for Eurydice

Orpheus, a famous musician and poet from Greek mythology, had a tragic love affair with Eurydice, who met a disastrous fate following a snake bite. Refusing to accept the loss of her love, Orpheus decided to descend to the Underworld, the realm of the dead, in hopes of bringing her back to life. Armed with his lyre and his exceptional talent, he managed to move the gods and creatures of the Underworld with his melodious music.

Hades, the god of the Underworld, touched by Orpheus' performance and determination, agreed to bring Eurydice back to life on one condition: Orpheus was not to turn to look at her until he had left the Underworld. Unfortunately, just before leaving the underworld, Orpheus, consumed by doubt, turned around, causing Eurydice's final loss.

This myth exemplifies themes of love, loss, and the power of music. It also reminds us of the dangers of doubt and impatience. The story of Orpheus and Eurydice continues to be told and reinterpreted in art and literature, testifying to its lasting impact on culture and the collective imagination.

This mythological episode underscores the idea that even in the face of death, love and art can prove to be incredibly powerful forces, capable of moving the most hardened hearts and defying the laws of nature.

Fact 24 - Arachnea Woven into a Spider by Athena

Arachnea, in Greek mythology, was a mortal maiden known for her exceptional weaving skills. She was so skilled that she claimed to be a better weaver than the goddess Athena herself, the protector of arts and crafts. Athena, offended by this arrogance, decided to confront her by taking on the appearance of an old woman to give her a lesson in humility and advise her to ask forgiveness for her pride.

Refusing to listen to the disguised goddess' advice, Arachnea persisted in her claim, pushing Athena to reveal herself and challenge her to a weaving contest. Each of them then wove a beautiful tapestry, reflecting their skill and creativity. However, Arachnea's weaving, while perfect, depicted the love affairs and deceptions of the gods, which angered Athena.

Enraged and feeling insulted, Athena destroyed Arachnea's tapestry and turned it into a spider, condemning it to eternally spin webs. This story is the origin of the word "arachnid" and serves as a warning against the pride and defiance of the gods, while celebrating the art of weaving and the mythical origins of a common creature in our daily lives.

Fact 25 - The Forbidden Love of Psyche and Eros

Psyche was a mortal of such striking beauty that she aroused the jealousy of Aphrodite, the goddess of love. Worried that Psyche would be worshipped more than she was, Aphrodite sent her son Eros, the god of love, to punish her. However, upon seeing Psyche, Eros fell madly in love with her and could not bring himself to carry out his mother's plan.

So Eros hid Psyche in a secret palace and came to see her every night, on the condition that she never try to see his face. Psyche, madly in love but tormented by doubt, gave in to temptation and lit up her lover's face as he slept, thus discovering his true identity. Eros, betrayed, flees, leaving Psyche in despair.

To find her lover, Psyche had to overcome several challenges imposed by Aphrodite, proving her determination and true love. Moved by her perseverance, Zeus, the king of the gods, intervened and granted immortality to Psyche, allowing her to live eternally with Eros.

Their story, like an ancient fairy tale, illustrates the universal themes of love, sacrifice and the pursuit of happiness, showing that even in mythology, love can triumph over the most insurmountable obstacles.

Fact 26 - Demeter's Revenge and Famine

Demeter, goddess of agriculture and fertility, went through a heartbreaking ordeal when her daughter Persephone was kidnapped by Hades, the god of the underworld. Enraged and devastated, Demeter refused to fulfill her divine duties, plunging the world into unprecedented famine. Crops were dying, and the once fertile land was turning into a barren desert.

The other gods, worried about the consequences of this famine on humanity and their own worship, tried to persuade Demeter to end her strike. However, she remained adamant, vowing never to restore the fertility of the land until she was reunited with her beloved daughter.

Eventually, Zeus, unable to ignore the desperate pleas of mortals, intervened and negotiated with Hades for Persephone's return. But there was one condition: Persephone was not to eat anything during her stay in the Underworld.

Unfortunately, Persephone had eaten six pomegranate seeds, condemning her to spend six months of each year in the Underworld and the other six months on Earth with her mother. Thus the cycle of the seasons was established, with winter corresponding to the period of Demeter's mourning and summer to their joyous reunion. This mythical story not only explains the changing of the seasons, but also illustrates the power of motherly love and its ability to turn the world upside down.

Fact 27 - Pygmalion falls in love with a statue

Pygmalion, a talented sculptor from the island of Cyprus, had a special vision of love and beauty. Tired of the deplorable behavior of the women of his time, he decided to devote himself entirely to his art. He then sculpted a statue of a woman so perfect and beautiful that it seemed almost alive. Pygmalion, moved by his own creation, fell madly in love with her.

He treated her like a true companion, giving her gifts, adorning her with jewels, and talking to her as if she could hear him. Despite the happiness he found in his company, Pygmalion suffered from the reality of the situation: he was in love with an inanimate statue. In his distress, he implored the goddess of love, Aphrodite, to give him a wife as perfect as his creation.

Aphrodite, touched by Pygmalion's sincere and selfless love, decided to grant her wish. She breathed life into the statue, turning cold marble into warm flesh. Pygmalion was dazzled to see his beloved come to life before his eyes.

This story also highlights the recurring theme of divine intervention as an answer to the sincere and profound prayers of mortals. Pygmalion and his statue, named Galatea, lived happily ever after and even had a son, proving that love can transcend all limits, even those of reality and matter.

Fact 28 - Prometheus, the Fire Thief for Humans

Prometheus, one of the Titans of Greek mythology, is famous for his shrewd intelligence and love for humans. Seeing that humans lived in darkness and cold, he made the bold decision to steal fire from the gods. Armed with his cunning, he stole fire from Olympus and gave it to humans, forever changing the course of their existence.

The gods of Olympus, especially Zeus, were furious at this transgression. They considered fire to be a divine privilege and that Prometheus had overstepped his bounds by giving it to mortals. As a result, Zeus decided to severely punish Prometheus for his act of rebellion.

Prometheus' punishment was terrible and exemplary. He was chained to a rock on Mount Caucasus, and an eagle was sent to devour his liver every day. His liver regenerated every night, making his suffering eternal and unbearable.

Despite the cruelty of his punishment, Prometheus' act is often interpreted as a symbol of resistance to authority and sacrifice for the well-being of others. He will go down in history as the Titan who dared to defy the gods to bring light and warmth to humans, emphasizing the importance of innovation and progress in ancient Greek culture.

Fact 29 - Apollo's Lyre That Charms Everyone

Apollo, one of the most revered gods in Greek mythology, was renowned for his exceptional talent in music. He was the god of music, poetry, the arts, and he wielded the lyre like no one else. His lyre, a gift from his brother Hermes, had the power to charm anyone who listened, mortal and immortal alike.

Apollo's music had the power to soothe souls and heal ailments. When he played his lyre, the mountains danced, the rivers stopped flowing, and all living things stood still to listen to him. He even used his music to calm the furious gods and to make difficult times more bearable.

His talent was such that he did not hesitate to defend his status as the best musician. One day, a satyr named Marsyas challenged him by claiming that he could play the flute better than he could. Apollo accepted the challenge, and as expected, he won hands down, proving once again his musical supremacy.

Apollo's lyre thus became a symbol of artistic perfection in ancient Greek culture. It is a reminder of the power of music to touch the soul, to transform sad moments into moments of joy, and to unite all beings around harmony and beauty.

Fact 30 - The Hyades, Nymphs Transformed into Stars

The Hyades, in Greek mythology, were a group of nymphs associated with rain and storm, and they have a special place in the starry sky. According to legend, these nymphs were the daughters of Atlas, the titan condemned to carry the sky on his shoulders, and the Oceanid goddess Pleione. They were also the sisters of the Pleiades, another group of nymphs turned into stars.

Their transformation into a constellation has a moving history. When their brother Hyas was killed by a lion or a boar, depending on the version, their grief was so deep that they turned into stars. Zeus, touched by their pain, placed them in the sky to immortalize their sorrow and brotherly love. They are now known as the constellation Hyades, located in Taurus.

The constellation Hyades is famous for its V-shape, which is easily spotted in the night sky. It is also close to the star Aldebaran, the brightest star in Taurus, although Aldebaran is not technically part of the Hyades. This constellation, visible from November to April in the Northern Hemisphere, is a constant reminder of the special place of myths and legends in ancient Greek astronomy.

The Hyades thus play a crucial role in connecting mythology, astronomy, and human emotions, showing how the ancient Greeks sought meaning and beauty even in the saddest moments.

Fact 31 - Hermès' winged sandals

Among the most famous attributes of Hermes, the messenger of the gods in Greek mythology, are his winged sandals, also known as talaria. These special shoes allowed him to move at an incredible speed, an indispensable asset for a god in charge of transmitting messages between heaven and earth. They are often depicted in art and literature as being made of gold, with small wings attached to the ankle or heel.

Legend has it that Hermes' winged sandals were made by Hephaestus, the blacksmith god. It was a gift from Zeus to his son Hermes to celebrate his appointment as messenger of the gods. In addition to their speed, these sandals also had the power to allow Hermes to walk on water and move through the air, emphasizing its role as a mediator between different worlds.

In addition to their practical utility, winged sandals have become a powerful symbol of speed and mobility. They are a reminder of Hermes' responsibilities as a guide of souls to the afterlife and his ability to move freely between the divine and mortal worlds. In addition, they symbolize his mischievous nature and his love of cunning, as they allowed him to get out of tricky situations with disconcerting speed.

Today, Hermès' winged sandals continue to inspire and fascinate, becoming a recognizable symbol of Greek mythology in popular culture.

Fact 32 - The War Between Athena and Poseidon for Athens

In ancient times, Athens, one of the most important cities in Greece, was the scene of intense competition between Athena, goddess of wisdom, and Poseidon, god of the sea. Everyone wanted to become the protector of the city and give it their name. The two deities offered a gift to the citizens, and the most useful gift was to determine the victor.

Poseidon struck the ground with his trident and caused a spring of salt water to gush out, a symbol of his power over the oceans and horses. Although impressive, this gift did not prove to be very useful to the inhabitants. Athena, on the other hand, offered an olive tree, a symbol of peace and prosperity. The Athenians considered his gift more valuable, as it brought them food, wood, and oil.

Thus, Athena won the competition, and the city took her name, becoming Athens. The olive tree offered by Athena was planted on the Acropolis, where it became an object of veneration and an enduring symbol of Athena's victory. The saltwater spring created by Poseidon has also become an attraction, known as the "sacred sea."

This episode not only illustrates the competitiveness between the Greek gods, but also highlights the values dear to the Athenians: wisdom, peace and prosperity. The Athena olive tree remains a powerful symbol of Greece and its rich mythological history to this day.

Fact 33 - Chimeras, Beasts with Many Faces

In Greek mythology, the chimera is a fascinating and terrifying creature that combines the traits of several different animals. Traditionally, she is described as having the body and head of a lion, with a second goat's head emerging from her back, and a tail that ends in the head of a snake. This creature embodies chaos and fear, being almost impossible to defeat due to its multiple forms.

The chimera has played a central role in various myths and legends, often as a formidable adversary that had to be defeated. Bellerophon, a hero from Greek mythology, is famous for fighting and killing the chimera, a feat he achieved by riding Pegasus, the winged horse. This battle has become one of the most iconic narratives in Greek mythology, symbolizing the struggle between order and chaos.

The legend of the chimera has endured through the centuries, and the creature itself has become a symbol of unbridled imagination and the impossible. In modern language, the term "chimera" is often used to describe something that is perceived as fanciful, unrealistic, or illusory.

This myth illustrates how the ancient Greeks used fantasy stories and mythical creatures to explain the world around them, while also conveying important lessons and cultural values.

Fact 34 - The Atalanta Race and the Golden Apples

Atalanta, a swift and skilled hunter from Greek mythology, is famous for participating in a race that defied the norms of her time. She had vowed to marry only the man who could beat her in the race, a seemingly impossible task given her exceptional speed. However, Hippomenes, a shrewd young man, rose to the challenge, armed with an ingenious plan.

To win the race and the heart of Atalanta, Hippomenes obtained three golden apples from the garden of the Hesperides, thanks to the help of the goddess Aphrodite. During the race, every time Atalanta started to get ahead of him, he threw a golden apple to distract her. Curious and seduced by the shiny apples, Atalante stopped to pick them, wasting precious time.

This tactic proved effective, allowing Hippomenes to win the race and Atalanta's hand. This myth illustrates not only cunning and intelligence, but also the power of love and persuasion. The story of Atalanta and Hippomenes remains one of the most captivating in Greek mythology, showing that sometimes brute force and speed are not enough, and that cleverness and cunning can prevail.

The myth of Atalanta and Hippomenes continues to be an example of how ingenuity and strategy can triumph in seemingly impossible situations, a lesson that is still relevant today.

Fact 35 - Aphrodite, born from the foam of the sea

The divine origin of Aphrodite, the Greek goddess of love and beauty, is as fascinating as it is unique in Greek mythology. Unlike many other gods and goddesses, Aphrodite was not born to two divine parents, but rather from the foam of the sea. According to legend, when Cronus cut off his father Uranus' genitals and threw them into the sea, the foam created by this act gave birth to Aphrodite.

Emerging from the sea in Cyprus, Aphrodite was received and clothed by the seasons, before being taken to Olympus. Her beauty was so extraordinary that she immediately captivated the attention of all the gods. To avoid the quarrels and conflicts caused by her charm, Zeus quickly married her to Hephaestus, the blacksmith of the gods.

Aphrodite played a crucial role in many Greek stories and myths, using her power of seduction to influence both gods and mortals. She is often depicted emerging from the sea, a scene that captures the essence of her divine and mysterious birth. Her story serves as a reminder of the power of beauty and love, central themes in Greek mythology that continue to inspire and fascinate people to this day.

Fact 36 - Theseus fights the Minotaur

Theseus' epic fight against the Minotaur is one of the most gripping stories in Greek mythology. Son of Aegeus, king of Athens, Theseus volunteered to be one of seven young men and seven young women sent as tribute to Minos, the king of Crete, to be devoured by the Minotaur. This half-man, half-bull monster was locked in the labyrinth designed by Daedalus, a trap from which no one could escape.

Upon her arrival in Crete, Minos' daughter Ariadne fell madly in love with Theseus. She offered him a ball of yarn and a sword to help him defeat the Minotaur and find his way through the maze. With these tools and his bravery, Theseus entered the labyrinth, found the Minotaur, and confronted him in mortal combat, which he won through his strength and determination.

After killing the Minotaur, Theseus used the ball of thread to find his way back out of the maze. His triumph symbolized the victory of order over chaos, and he became a hero to the Athenian people. This story highlights the importance of bravery, intelligence and sacrifice in the pursuit of good, values dear to ancient Greek culture.

Fact 37 - Orpheus' Magic Harp

Orpheus, son of the god Apollo and the muse Calliope, was gifted with exceptional musical talent, inherited from his divine lineage. He played the lyre, a stringed instrument, with such mastery and passion that even the natural elements and wild creatures stood still to listen to him. His music had the power to charm everything around him, creating a moment of peace and universal harmony.

When Orpheus lost his love, Eurydice, bitten by a snake and sent to the Underworld, decided to descend into the realm of the dead to bring her back. Armed with his lyre and his courage, he managed to appease the terrifying creatures and soften the hearts of the gods of the Underworld with his melodies. His music touched Hades and Persephone so much that they agreed to let Eurydice go, on condition that Orpheus would not turn around until he had reached daylight, a condition that he unfortunately could not respect.

Orpheus' harp has gone down in mythology as a symbol of the transformative power of art and love. She is a reminder that even in the darkest of times, beauty and perseverance can open unexpected doors and touch the most hardened hearts. This story teaches the power of faith and the sometimes tragic consequences of impatience.

Fact 38 - The Moires Who Spin Destiny

In Greek mythology, the Moires were three divine sisters responsible for spinning the fate of gods and mortals. They were daughters of the Night or, according to other versions, of Zeus and Themis. Their role was crucial, as they had the power to determine the length of each being's life and the course of their existence.

The first, Clotho, was the one who spun life, deciding when each being came into the world. The second, Lachesis, measured the length of the thread of life, thus determining the length of each individual's existence. The third, Atropos, was the most feared, as she had the power to cut the thread of life, ending existence.

The Moires were uncompromising and impartial, making no distinction between mortals and immortals. Even the gods feared and respected them, for they knew that they were subject to their authority. The inevitability of the fate spun by the Moires is a recurring theme in Greek literature and philosophy, reminding everyone that life is precious, but also fragile and ephemeral.

Fact 39 - Midas and Everything He Touches Turns Gold

Midas, famous king of Phrygia in Greek mythology, is best known for his ability to turn anything he touched into gold. This faculty was granted to him by Dionysus, the god of wine and feasting, as a token of gratitude for Midas' hospitality to one of his followers. Dazzled by the prospect of infinite riches, Midas did not immediately grasp the consequences of this gift.

The king quickly realized the extent of his mistake. His food, his drink, and even his own daughter turned to pure gold at the slightest touch. Desperate and hungry, Midas begged Dionysus to take away the gift-turned-curse. Touched by the king's distress, the god agreed and showed him how to get rid of this power by bathing in the river Pactolus, whose sands then became glittering with gold.

This episode in Midas' life serves as a warning against greed and reminds us that material wealth, no matter how abundant, cannot replace the simple joys of life and human connections. The story of Midas has become a timeless parable, vividly illustrating that there are far more precious things than gold.

Fact 40 - Medea's Revenge on Jason

Medea, a tragic and complex figure in Greek mythology, is famous for her ruthless revenge on Jason, the leader of the Argonauts. After helping Jason conquer the Golden Fleece with his sorcery skills, Medea expected a lifetime of happiness by his side. However, reality took a dark turn when Jason betrayed her, choosing to marry another woman to cement his power and status.

Medea, devastated and enraged by this betrayal, has concocted a diabolical plan of revenge. She sent Jason's new wife a poisoned gift that led to his and her father's gruesome death. But Medea's revenge didn't stop there.

In a final act of devastation, Medea killed her own children, born of her union with Jason, to inflict the latter the greatest of pains. This dramatic and shocking gesture has marked history as one of the most extreme and unforgettable revenges in Greek mythology.

The story of Medea and her revenge is a poignant reminder of the dangers of betrayal and the dark depths to which anger and pain can lead. She remains an iconic figure in mythology, symbolizing both female power and the devastating consequences of unchecked anger.

Fact 41 - The Sharp Claws of the Sphinx

The Sphinx, a mythical creature with a woman's head and a lion's body, is best known for its riddles and its crucial role in the story of Oedipus. This feared monster terrorized the city of Thebes, posing a riddle to travelers and killing those who could not answer it. His presence created an atmosphere of fear and despair among the Thebans.

The sharp claws of the Sphinx were one of its most feared attributes. She used them to instantly attack and kill those who failed to solve her riddle. These claws were the embodiment of the mortal threat she posed to the city.

Oedipus, the future king of Thebes, was the only one to solve the riddle of the Sphinx. His intelligence and insight put an end to the days of terror imposed by the creature, causing him to commit suicide by throwing himself off a cliff. This victory not only saved Thebes, but also elevated Oedipus to heroism.

The story of the Sphinx emphasizes the importance of intelligence and cunning in the face of seemingly insurmountable challenges. It remains a powerful symbol of the intellectual obstacle, reminding us that sometimes mental strength can triumph where physical strength fails.

Fact 42 - The Maden Dance

The Maenads, also known as the Bacchae, were the exalted followers of the god Dionysus in Greek mythology, famous for their wild dances and ecstatic rituals. They embodied total devotion and self-abandonment, completely losing themselves in the celebration of their god. Their intense and frenetic dancing was a sight that was both fascinating and terrifying.

These women, often described as being in a trance-like state, engaged in ecstatic activities that defied social norms. They danced until they were exhausted, screaming and singing in a state of ecstatic joy. Their movements were so swift and uncontrolled that they seemed to be possessed by a divine force.

The Maenads played a central role in the cult of Dionysus, participated in mystical rituals, and were the protagonists of many mythological stories. Their dancing was not only a form of devotion, but also a way to connect with the divine, transcend the mortal world, and attain a state of spiritual grace.

Their legacy lives on in art and literature, where they are often depicted as figures of freedom and unconstrained expression. They are a reminder of the transformative power of music and dance, and the ability of art to awaken the deepest passions of the soul.

Fact 43 - Hades' Invisibility Helmet

Hades' invisibility helmet is one of the most intriguing objects in Greek mythology, granting the wearer the ability to make themselves invisible. According to legends, this artifact was forged by the Cyclops and given to Hades, the god of the underworld, during the titanic war between the gods and the Titans. He played a crucial role in the victory of the Olympian gods, allowing Hades to move unseen and surprise the enemy.

This helmet was not only used by Hades; It was also loaned to other gods and heroes when they needed it. For example, Perseus used it to defeat the Gorgon Medusa, a creature whose gaze could turn men to stone. Thanks to the helmet, Perseus was able to approach Medusa undetected and cut off her head.

The idea of an object conferring invisibility has captivated the human imagination for millennia, and Hades' invisibility helmet is a great example of how this idea was already present in ancient times. This artifact exemplifies the creativity and ingenuity of Greek myths, offering a fantastic solution to heroic challenges.

Today, Hades' invisibility helmet continues to fascinate and inspire, serving as a reminder of the power of imagination and the enduring influence of Greek mythology on modern culture. The stories surrounding this mythical object underscore the value of cunning and ingenuity, universal themes that still resonate today.

Fact 44 - The Fall of Icarus Too Close to the Sun

The Fall of Icarus is one of the most poignant and instructive stories in Greek mythology, illustrating the dangers of excess. Icarus, son of Daedalus, a genius inventor and architect, found himself locked with his father in the Labyrinth of Crete, an intricate structure designed by Daedalus himself. To escape, Daedalus made wings for himself and his son, using feathers and wax.

Before taking flight, Daedalus warns Icarus not to fly too close to the sun, nor too low near the sea. However, dazzled by the excitement of flying, Icarus forgot his father's advice. It rose into the sky, closer and closer to the sun, until the wax that held its wings together began to melt.

The feathers came loose, leaving Icarus with no way to support himself in the air. He fell into the sea and drowned, leaving behind an eternal lesson about the risks of excess and the importance of listening and caution. The place of its fall was later named the Icarian Sea, a permanent tribute to its tragic history.

The story of Icarus continues to captivate and serve as a warning, reminding future generations of the potentially devastating consequences of pride and disobedience. She embodies the Greek ideal of "metron ariston," or "measure is best," emphasizing the value of balance and moderation in all things.

Fact 45 - Calydon's Gigantic Boar Hunt

The Hunt for the Boar of Calydon is an epic adventure from Greek mythology, orchestrated by King Oeneus of Calydon. After neglecting to pay homage to the goddess Artemis at an annual sacrifice, Oeneus found herself facing divine wrath. In retaliation, Artemis sent a gigantic boar to ravage the lands of Calydon, destroying crops and spreading terror.

Faced with this threat, Oeneus gathered the greatest heroes of Greece for a massive hunt. Among them were legendary figures such as Achilles, Odysseus, and Atalanta, the only woman in this heroic group. Atalanta, a fearsome hunter, played a crucial role in the hunt, being the first to injure the ferocious beast.

Calydon's wild boar hunt was not only a display of bravery and skill, but also a defining moment for Atalanta. She proved that a woman could stand equal to men, even in the most perilous situations. His participation made an impression and demonstrated that courage and competence know no gender.

The epic tale of Calydon's wild boar hunt remains etched in the collective memory as an example of heroic defiance and divine justice. It is a reminder of the values of courage, skill and equality, while illustrating the severe consequences that can result from forgetting religious duties.

Fact 46 - The Nereids, Nymphs of the Seas

The Nereids are enchanting sea deities from Greek mythology, daughters of Nereus, the old god of the sea, and Doris, an Oceanid. Fifty of them inhabit the depths of the Aegean Sea, in a sumptuous palace surrounded by coral gardens and marine fauna. Their grace and beauty are legendary, and they are often depicted riding sea creatures, dressed in flowing robes and adorned with jewels.

Their role in Greek mythology is varied, but they are particularly known for their ability to help sailors in distress. A famous example is their intervention to support Achilles during the Trojan War. Thetis, one of the Nereids, is his mother, and she plays a crucial role in several key moments in the Homeric epic.

Nereids are also associated with love and fertility, and they are often invoked in marriage rites. Their influence extends even beyond the seas, as evidenced by the myth of Galatea, a Nereid who fell in love with a mortal.

As you delve into the tales of Greek mythology, you'll discover the importance of the Nereids in the ancient imagination. Their presence emphasizes the deep connection between the ancient Greeks and the marine world, and their worship reflects admiration and respect for the mysterious forces of nature.

Fact 47 - Poseidon's trident that makes the earth shake

The trident, a three-pronged weapon, is the ultimate emblem of Poseidon, the powerful god of the sea in Greek mythology. It is not merely a weapon or ornament, but a symbol of his power and authority over the oceans and everything in them. With this trident, Poseidon could not only control waves and unleash storms, but also cause earthquakes, emphasizing his connection with telluric forces.

A famous episode illustrating the power of the trident is found in the Odyssey, when Poseidon, furious with Odysseus, raises gigantic waves to hinder his return to Ithaca. The sea is agitated and the sky darkens, demonstrating the wrath of the god and the phenomenal power of his trident.

The trident is so associated with Poseidon that his image has become synonymous with the god himself. In Greek art and sculpture, Poseidon is frequently depicted holding his trident tightly, ready to hurl his powers upon the world.

Thus, throughout Greek mythology, Poseidon's trident serves not only as a reminder of the god's sovereignty over the oceans, but also of his terrifying power capable of shaking the earth itself. It symbolizes the close connection between the gods of Olympus and the natural elements, and how these divine forces can influence the lives of mortals.

Fact 48 - The Dreams Sent by Morpheus

Morpheus, the Greek god of dreams, possesses a fascinating and mysterious power in the mythological universe. He has the unique ability to take on any human form and appear in mortals' dreams, sending messages from the gods or simply influencing the events of the waking world. His dream appearances are often described as incredibly realistic and vivid, leaving those who experience them in a state of amazement or deep contemplation.

One of the most famous examples of Morpheus' influence is his role in Homer's "Iliad," where he appears in a dream to deliver a crucial message. He takes the form of one of Agamemnon's companions, the king of the Achaeans, and pushes him to resume the fight against Troy, thus changing the course of the war.

Morpheus is often depicted carrying a poppy, a flower associated with sleep and dreams, and holding a branch that has the power to lull anyone who touches it to sleep. These symbols emphasize his connection to the dream world and his power to manipulate states of consciousness.

Addressing this message directly to you, the reader, it is fascinating to think about the influence that Morpheus might have on our own dreams. Imagine if, as the ancient Greeks believed, our dreams were messages from the gods, shaped and delivered by Morpheus himself.

Fact 49 - The Heavy Weight of Sisyphus to Roll Forever

Greek mythology is filled with stories of eternal punishment, and the myth of Sisyphus is one of the most iconic. A cunning and deceitful king, Sisyphus ended up angering the gods with his arrogance and ability to outwit death. As a result, he was condemned to a task that was both simple and infinitely difficult: rolling a huge boulder to the top of a hill, only to see it come down again each time, for eternity.

This punishment, decided by Zeus himself, symbolizes the futility and repetitive nature of certain tasks in life. Sisyphus' hard work never leads to fulfillment or success, creating a powerful metaphor about the absurdity of life and human endeavors.

The story of Sisyphus has been interpreted in various ways over time, becoming a popular topic in philosophy and literature. Albert Camus, for example, used the story of Sisyphus as an analogy for the search for meaning in human life, emphasizing the perseverance required to keep going despite the seeming absurdity of our efforts.

As I tell you this story, it's impossible not to wonder about the "rocks" we push into our own lives. Sisyphus reminds us to find our own meaning and persevere, even when the path seems endless and meaningless.

Fact 50 - Zeus' tricks to seduce

Zeus, the king of the gods in Greek mythology, was known for his many love affairs, often tinged with cunning and metamorphosis. To seduce those he desired, Zeus did not hesitate to use subterfuge, transforming his appearance or that of the object of his desires. These stories reflect the complexity of the relationship between gods and mortals, as well as themes of power and desire.

A famous example is the abduction of Europa, where Zeus transformed into a white bull to attract the attention of the beautiful Phoenician princess. Amazed by the animal's gentleness, Europa climbed on its back, and Zeus took the opportunity to take it to the island of Crete. This story highlights the cunning and ingenuity of Zeus, who is able to manipulate situations to his advantage.

In another adventure, Zeus took on the appearance of a swan to seduce Leda, the queen of Sparta. The depiction of Zeus as a swan falling in love with Leda has become a recurring artistic motif in art and literature.

These stories, while they may seem strange or even shocking through the lens of modern values, are fundamental elements of Greek mythology, shedding light on the capricious and unpredictable nature of the gods. They remind us that, in the world of mythology, power and desire were often intertwined, and that the gods, although divine, were not exempt from human passions.

Fact 51 - The Fury of Hera, Jealous of Zeus' Love

Hera, the wife of Zeus and queen of the gods, is famous in Greek mythology for her fiery jealousy. His wrath fell not only on Zeus, but also on the many illegitimate mistresses and children of the supreme god. Hera never tolerated her husband's infidelities, although they were many and varied, ranging from mere mortals to other deities.

A striking example is that of Heracles, the son of Zeus and the mortal Alcmene. Hera, in her anger, sent two snakes to kill the baby in its cradle, but the young Heracles choked them with his own hands. This illustrates Hera's determination to punish the offspring of Zeus' infidelities, regardless of their innocence.

Leto, another lover of Zeus, also suffered the wrath of Hera. Pregnant with twins, Zeus turned Leto into a quail to protect her, but Hera sent the serpent Python to pursue her relentlessly. This story highlights Hera's persistence and resentment in the face of Zeus' infidelity.

Hera, in her quest for vengeance, often used cruel and violent stratagems, leaving indelible traces in Greek mythology. His reactions illustrate the complexity of the relationship between the gods and highlight the earthly consequences of divine quarrels. These stories, though ancient, continue to captivate with their dramatic intensity and depth of emotion.

Fact 52 - The Gorgoneion, Athena's Fearsome Shield

The gorgoneion is one of the most iconic attributes of the goddess Athena, daughter of Zeus and goddess of wisdom, war, and strategy. This term refers to a representation of the head of Medusa, one of the three Gorgons, attached to the center of Athena's shield. Medusa, with her snake hair and petrifying gaze, was turned into a monster by Athena herself, after being seduced into her temple by Poseidon.

This shield is not just an element of defense; it is also a psychological weapon, instilling fear and terror in enemies who dare to meet the Gorgon's gaze. Athena used it many times, most notably during the Trojan War, to protect Greek heroes and instill fear among the Trojans.

The gorgoneion isn't just found on Athena's shield. It was widely used in Greek art and architecture, often as a protective talisman. It can be found on pottery, mosaics, and even coinage, attesting to its importance in ancient Greek culture and religion.

As a symbol of protection and power, Athena's gorgoneion remains one of the most powerful and intriguing images in Greek mythology. It bears witness to the complexity of religious beliefs and practices of the time, blending art, religion and society in a rich carpet of traditions and myths.

Fact 53 - The Twelve Labors Imposed on Hercules

Hercules, the legendary hero of Greek mythology, is famous for his twelve labors, imposed by King Eurystheus. These feats were a form of penance after Hercules, in a fit of madness sent by Hera, killed his wife and children. These works were supposed to be so difficult that they seemed impossible to achieve, testing Hercules' strength, courage, and intelligence.

Among these tasks were tasks such as defeating the Nemean lion, whose skin was impenetrable, or capturing the Cerynian deer, an animal so fast that it seemed impossible to catch. Each job had its own unique challenge, forcing Hercules to use both his brute strength and ingenuity.

By completing these works, Hercules became a symbol of bravery and strength in Greek mythology, with his story told through the generations. These stories have served to instill values of perseverance and resilience, showing that with enough determination, even the toughest tasks can be accomplished.

Today, the story of the Twelve Labours of Hercules continues to capture the imagination, reflecting the heroic ideal of ancient Greece and leaving a lasting legacy in Western culture. The exploits of Hercules are an eternal reminder that no matter the challenges, strength and courage can lead to victory.

Fact 54 - The Mysterious Oracle of Delphi

The Oracle of Delphi, also known as the Pythia, was one of the most important and respected oracles of ancient Greece, located on the slopes of Mount Parnassus. People came from all over to consult the Pythia, Apollo's priestess, hoping for advice and predictions for the future. It was believed that the Pythia was able to communicate directly with Apollo and receive prophetic visions from the god.

The process of consulting the oracle was complex and mysterious. The Pythia would go into a trance, often induced by the fumes that emanated from a crack in the ground, and utter enigmatic words that were then interpreted by the temple priests. These responses were notorious for being ambiguous and enigmatic, forcing those who consulted them to think deeply about their meaning.

The influence of the Delphic oracle extended far beyond the borders of Greece, influencing the decisions of rulers and ordinary citizens. Famous examples of consultations include King Croesus of Lydia, who misinterpreted a prophecy, leading to his downfall, and Socrates, whose reputation as a sage was enhanced by the words of the Pythia.

Today, the oracle of Delphi is considered a fascinating example of how religion and mysticism influenced daily life in antiquity.

Fact 55 - Niobe's Revenge Turned into a Rock

Niobe, queen of Thebes, was famous for her beauty and inordinate pride, boasting of having more children and being happier than the goddess Leto herself. She loudly proclaimed that her seven sons and seven daughters, the Niobids, were far superior to Apollo and Artemis, the children of Leto. Enraged by this arrogance, Leto sent her children to punish Niobe in a tragic and ruthless manner.

Apollo and Artemis, skilled archers, shot their arrows with deadly accuracy, killing all the children of Niobe in a single day. In the face of such loss, Niobe was consumed by grief and pain, unable to find comfort. Her heart froze and she was turned into a rock from which eternal tears flowed, a poignant image of her inconsolable sorrow.

This story is a stark reminder of the importance of respect for the gods in Greek mythology, highlighting the tragic consequences of pride and vanity. The ruins of Thebes and the weeping rock of Niobe remain silent witnesses to this legend, captivating the imagination of visitors and recalling the weight of words and deeds in the ancient world.

Fact 56 - Hundred-eyed Argos watches over Io

In Greek mythology, Argos is a unique creature with a hundred eyes. His vigilance was so renowned that the king of the gods, Zeus, assigned him to a task of the utmost importance: watching over Io. Io was a nymph, and Zeus, in love with her, had turned her into a heifer to protect her from the jealousy of his wife, Hera. But Hera, cunning and suspicious, asked Argos to keep an eye on Io, fully understanding her husband's intentions.

Argos carried out his task with formidable efficiency, always keeping at least one eye open, making any attempt at escape or rescue impossible. His dedication was such that it was an insurmountable obstacle for anyone who wanted to approach the heifer.

However, Zeus could not sit idly by and sent Hermes, the messenger of the gods, to free Io. Hermes used his charm and cunning to lull Argos to sleep, before killing him, thus ending his relentless surveillance. The legend of Argos of the Hundred Eyes serves as a powerful reminder of vigilance and loyalty, but also of the gods' ability to use cunning to achieve their goals.

Fact 57 - Penelope's Magic Tapestry

Penelope, the wife of Odysseus, remained famous in Greek mythology for her ingenuity and loyalty to her husband, who left for the Trojan War. During her absence, many suitors invaded her palace, urging her to choose a new husband. To keep them at bay, Penelope devised an ingenious scheme related to her loom.

She promised to choose a suitor once her tapestry was completed, a work dedicated to her father-in-law, Laertes. However, each night, in secret, she undid some of the work done during the day, thus prolonging the making of the tapestry indefinitely. This ruse allowed him to remain loyal to Odysseus and gain time while waiting for his return.

Penelope's trick became a symbol of female cunning and marital loyalty in ancient mythology and literature. Her determination to preserve her marriage and her ability to manipulate suitors reveal a strong and resourceful woman, capable of cunning the male heroes of her time.

Eventually, Odysseus returned, and after demonstrating his true identity and driving away the suitors, he was able to find his faithful wife. The story of Penelope and her tapestry continues to fascinate and inspire, shining a light on the power of intelligence and perseverance in the face of adversity.

Fact 58 - The Argonauts in Search of the Golden Fleece

The Argonauts' expedition is one of the most fascinating adventures in Greek mythology. Under Jason's command, a group of heroes set out on a perilous journey to Colchis in search of the Golden Fleece. This precious object was supposed to secure for Jason the throne of Iolcos, usurped by his uncle Pelias.

The Argo, the ship that gave its name to the Argonauts, was built by Argos, and it had the particularity of having a beam from the sacred oak of Dodona, capable of rendering oracles. The crew was made up of legendary figures, such as Heracles, Orpheus, and the Dioscuri, each bringing their skills and bravery to the group.

Their quest led them to overcome countless trials, including the perilous passage between the Symplegades rocks and the clash with the warriors born from the dragon's teeth sown by Jason. Medea, the daughter of the king of Colchis, fell in love with Jason and helped him complete his quest, thus betraying her own father.

The Golden Fleece was eventually taken away by Jason, thanks to Medea's precious help. This heroic feat remains etched in the collective memory as a testament to courage, ingenuity and perseverance, perfectly illustrating the adventurous and epic spirit of Greek mythology.

Fact 59 - Tithon's Fountain of Youth

The story of Tithon and the goddess of dawn, Eos, is one of the most poignant tales in Greek mythology. Eos, madly in love with the mortal Tithon, had him kidnapped and taken to the end of the world, where the sun rises. In the face of his infinite love, she begged Zeus to make Tithon immortal, a favor that the king of the gods gladly granted.

However, Eos made a crucial mistake by failing to also ask for eternal youth for his beloved. With time, Tithon grew inexorably old, losing his beauty and vigor, while Eos remained eternally young. The contrast between his eternal youth and Tithon's decrepitude became more and more striking as the years passed.

In the face of this tragedy, a devastated Eos, finally transformed Tithon into a cicada, a symbol of longevity and renewal. This sad fate is a cruel reminder of the dangers and unintended consequences that misformulated wishes in Greek mythology can have.

The story of Tithon and Eos serves as a cautionary tale, illustrating that even the gifts of the gods can have unintended consequences. It emphasizes the importance of precision and clarity in our desires and aspirations, a timeless teaching passed down through the ages.

Fact 60 - The Unleashed Breath of the Aeolus Winds

In Greek mythology, Aeolus is known as the guardian and master of the winds, a crucial role in a world where navigation was at the heart of civilization. Based on the floating island of Aeolia, he controlled the winds with unparalleled power, being able to calm or unleash them at will. The gods himself consulted him and feared him, knowing well the extent of his influence.

Homer's Odyssey offers a striking example of Aeolus' intervention in human affairs. Odysseus, on his way back to Ithaca, stopped at the island of Aeolia. Impressed by the hero, Aeolus offered him a bag containing all the headwinds, leaving only the favorable wind to bring Odysseus home.

However, Odysseus' companions, believing that the bag contained treasure, opened it prematurely, thus releasing all winds and once again driving Odysseus away from his homeland. This mishap illustrates not only the power of the winds under Aeolus' tutelage, but also the consequences of curiosity and ignorance.

The story of Aeolus and Odysseus reveals the capricious and unpredictable nature of the winds, as well as their far-reaching impact on navigation and the destiny of men. It also emphasizes the need for wisdom and prudence in all endeavors, reminding sailors and travelers to respect the forces of nature and the gifts of the gods.

Fact 61 - Hermes' tricks to deceive Argos

Argos, a hundred-eyed giant, is a fascinating character in Greek mythology. His peculiarity was that he could sleep while keeping some of his eyes open, making him the ideal guardian. Hera, jealous of Zeus' love affair with Io, turned the latter into a heifer and entrusted Argos with the task of watching over her relentlessly.

Hermes, the messenger of the gods, was sent by Zeus to free Io. Known for his ingenuity and quick wit, Hermes used his legendary cunning to deceive Argos. He began by numbing all his eyes by telling her boring stories and playing the lyre. Argos, unable to resist the soporific charm of Hermes' music and voice, fell asleep completely.

With Argos asleep, Hermes took the opportunity to cut off his head, freeing Io from his constant surveillance. This fact demonstrates not only Hermes' cunning, but also his crucial role as a facilitator of Zeus' designs, proving that with ingenuity, even the most formidable obstacles can be overcome.

The story of Hermes and Argos illustrates finesse and cunning as essential elements in solving complex problems, highlighting the importance of strategy and insight in Greek myths.

Fact 62 - The Northern Lights, Aurora Dances

The Northern Lights, the spectacular luminous phenomenon visible in the polar regions, have always aroused wonder and admiration. In Greek mythology, they were associated with the Auroras, the goddesses of the morning. These lights in the sky were believed to be the result of their celestial dance, creating a mesmerizing spectacle to celebrate the beginning of a new day.

Eos, the goddess of the dawn, is often depicted in mythological accounts as bringing daylight with her horse-drawn chariot. She dispels the darkness and welcomes the sun, her brother Helios, to the horizon. The Northern Lights were therefore interpreted as an extension of her power and beauty, lighting up the sky with bright, ethereal colors.

These natural phenomena were also seen as a bridge between the earthly and divine worlds, emphasizing the close connection between nature and mythology in ancient Greek culture. The auroras were a constant reminder of the presence of the gods and their influence on the world.

Thus, when observing the Northern Lights, the ancient Greeks saw in it the divine touch of Eos and her sisters, creating a moment of spiritual connection and wonder at the beauty and power of nature.

Fact 63 - Samson's strength, given by Zeus

It is important to note at the outset a common confusion in mythological accounts: Samson is actually a biblical figure, not a character from Greek mythology. He is famous for his prodigious strength, which comes from his long, uncut hair. However, it's easy to mix the stories and origins of myths across different cultures.

In Greek mythology, it is Heracles (or Hercules in Roman mythology) who is renowned for his superhuman strength. The son of Zeus, the king of the gods, and a mortal woman, Heracles possesses incredible strength and endurance, and he is best known for completing the Twelve Labors, near-impossible tasks that demonstrate his power.

One of the most fascinating aspects of Greek mythology is how stories and characters can transcend cultural boundaries, intertwining and transforming over time. Distinguishing origins from myths is essential to better understand their meanings and implications.

Thus, although Samson's strength is a central element of his story, it is not attributed to Zeus, but to God in the Judeo-Christian tradition. Heracles' strength, on the other hand, is a gift from his divine father, Zeus, in Greek mythology.

Fact 64 - The Secrets of Mount Olympus

Mount Olympus, Greece's legendary peak, is much more than just a geographical wonder. According to Greek mythology, it is the home of the twelve main gods, the very heart of divine activity. Perched at 2917 meters above sea level, its summit was considered inaccessible to mortals, shrouded in clouds and mysteries. Zeus, the king of the gods, held his throne there, and from there he could observe the world and hurl his dreaded thunderbolts.

Mount Olympus was also the place where the gods gathered to discuss the fate of mortals and the universe. It was a place of feasts and banquets, where nectar and ambrosia, the divine foods, were consumed. The gods lived there in palaces made of gold and precious stones, illustrating their power and wealth.

Despite its celestial status, Mount Olympus was also connected to the earth. The gods regularly descended from their abode to interfere in human affairs, making Mount Olympus central in many mythological tales. It was a place where heaven and earth met, symbolizing the connection between the divine and the mortal.

Today, Mount Olympus is a popular destination for hikers and nature lovers. Its history and majesty continue to fascinate, reminiscent of a time when gods walked among men and the world was full of magic and mystery.

Fact 65 - The Musical Challenge Between Pan and Apollo

When we talk about music in Greek mythology, two figures often stand out: Apollo, god of music, and Pan, god of fields and woods. One day, these two divine entities embarked on a musical challenge, each convinced of his superiority. Pan, with his pan flute, and Apollo, with his lyre, played music with such passion that it attracted the attention of the other gods.

The contest was held on Mount Parnassus, and King Midas was chosen as the judge. Pan played first, producing joyful, dancing sounds that captivated all the spectators. Then Apollo took up his lyre and played a melody so pure and melancholy that even the birds fell silent to listen.

When the performances ended, Midas declared Pan the winner, which angered Apollo. Sensing that the judgment was unfair and skewed by partiality, Apollo decided to punish Midas by giving him donkey ears, a heavy sentence to remind Midas of his error in judgment.

This story illustrates not only the power and importance of music in Greek mythology, but also the vanity of the gods and the severe consequences that could come from questioning their talent and superiority. It reminds us that in the world of the gods, pride and presumption could sometimes lead to unexpected and spectacular outcomes.

Fact 66 - The Wrath of Zeus Turns Lycaon into a Wolf

In the rich pantheon of Greek mythology, stories of divine transformations and punishments are commonplace. A striking example is that of Lycaon, a cruel king of Arcadia who dared to defy Zeus himself. According to legend, Lycaon did not believe in the divinity of Zeus when he came to visit his kingdom in human form. To test the god, Lycaon decided to serve him a meal made from the flesh of one of his own sons.

Zeus, who is not easily deceived, immediately understood the deception. Enraged by this unholy and cruel act, he decided to punish Lycaon severely. In a fit of divine rage, Zeus turned Lycaon into a wolf, condemning him to wander eternally in that form. Lycaon's son, who had been killed and served as a meal, was resurrected by Zeus, thus showing his power and ability to give and take back life.

This story, in addition to being a fascinating narrative, conveys a powerful message about the omnipotence of the gods and the terrible consequences that can come from defying them. It also illustrates the belief in divine justice and eternal punishment for those who commit immoral acts, a recurring theme in many mythologies.

Fact 67 - The Incredible Adventures of Perseus

Perseus, son of Zeus and the mortal Danaë, is a legendary hero of Greek mythology whose exploits are among the most daring and fantastical. His most famous quest was to decapitate the Gorgon Medusa, a terrifying creature whose gaze could turn anyone to stone. Armed with the gods' gifts, including a shining shield given to him by Athena and Hermes' winged sandals, Perseus managed to overcome the most difficult trials.

His cunning and courage helped him defeat Medusa by using the reflection in her shield to look at her without being turned to stone. After cutting off his head, Perseus used his head, which retained its petrifying power, as a formidable weapon. On his way home, he rescued and married Princess Andromeda, who was destined to be sacrificed to a sea monster.

Perseus' story doesn't end there. He also played a key role in the founding of Mycenae, one of the great cities of Greek antiquity, by throwing Medusa's head into a field where it landed, creating an army of stone soldiers. This adventure, full of magic, bravery and divine intervention, remains one of the most captivating sagas in Greek mythology, teaching lessons about the importance of intelligence and courage in conquering adversity.

Fact 68 - Aphrodite's Beauty Bath

Aphrodite, the Greek goddess of love and beauty, is famous for her divine beauty rituals, contributing to her eternally seductive appearance. According to mythology, she regularly took baths in seawater to preserve her youth and irresistible charm. These baths were not ordinary, as they were imbued with the magic and power of the gods, thus enhancing his seductive aura and magnetism.

The story goes that, born from the foam of the sea, Aphrodite had an innate connection with the aquatic elements, which enhanced the effectiveness of her sea baths. She emerged from each bath rejuvenated, her beauty magnified and her radiance revived, dazzling mortal and immortal.

In addition to her sea bathing, Aphrodite used various divine herbs and oils, imparting enchanted properties to maintain her youth and beauty. These elixirs were concocted with the utmost care, using rare and precious ingredients, fit for a goddess. These Aphrodite beauty practices emphasize the importance of self-care and beauty preservation through dedicated rituals and respect for natural gifts.

Such was her influence that, throughout ancient Greece, ritual baths inspired by Aphrodite's practices were incorporated into beauty routines, and many sought to emulate her secrets to capture a fraction of her eternal splendor.

Fact 69 - The Punishment of Thirsty Tantalus

Tantalus, a character in Greek mythology, is famous for the severe punishment inflicted on him by the gods of Olympus. Son of Zeus and the nymph Plouto, Tantalus was a mortal favored by the gods, but his pride and recklessness led to his downfall. He committed the reprehensible act of serving his own son, Pelops, as a feast to the gods, testing their omniscience. Horrified, the gods punished Tantalus by condemning him to spend eternity in Tartarus, a region of the Underworld.

There, Tantalus was plunged into a lake, the water almost reaching his lips, but every time he bent down to drink, the water receded, leaving him eternally thirsty. Above him, fruit-laden branches hung down, but they lifted out of reach as soon as he tried to grab them, leaving him hungry. This punishment was a ruthless reminder of his actions and a manifestation of divine justice in Greek mythology.

The myth of Tantalus illustrates the recurring theme of hubris, hubris and the serious consequences that flow from it. It serves as a warning against deception and disrespect towards deities, emphasizing the need to remain humble and respectful. The story of thirsty Tantalus continues to resonate, reminding us of the dangers of pride and impiety, and the need to live according to moral and respectful principles.

Fact 70 - Andromeda's prowess against a monster

Andromeda, a Greek mythological figure, is famous for the heroic story of her rescue by Perseus. Daughter of Cepheus and Cassiopeia, king and queen of Ethiopia, she found herself at the center of a tragedy due to her mother's arrogance. Cassiopeia had proclaimed that she and her daughter were more beautiful than the Nereids, nymphs of the sea, provoking the wrath of Poseidon, the god of the sea.

As punishment, Poseidon sent a sea monster to ravage the kingdom. An oracle declared that the only way to save the country was to sacrifice Andromeda to the monster. Bound to a rock, she awaited her fate when Perseus arrived, returning from his quest to decapitate the Gorgon Medusa.

Using Medusa's head, Perseus petrified the monster, saving Andromeda. She became his wife, proving that even in the darkest of times, heroism and courage can prevail. This story is a powerful reminder of the themes of bravery, sacrifice, and love in Greek mythology, showing how heroic deeds can overcome seemingly insurmountable odds.

Fact 71 - Athena's Protection of the City of Athens

The city of Athens, the epicenter of ancient Greek civilization, owes its name and protection to the goddess Athena. In the distant past, a conflict broke out between Athena and Poseidon, each wishing to be the protector of the city and give it their name. Their rivalry was such that the other Olympian gods decided to hold a contest to end the dispute.

Poseidon struck the ground with his trident, causing a spring of salt water to gush out, a sign of his power as the god of the sea. Athena, on the other hand, offered an olive tree, a symbol of peace and prosperity. The citizens, impressed by Athena's wisdom and generosity, chose the goddess as their protector, naming their city in her honor.

Since then, Athena has been revered as the protector of Athens, watching over its inhabitants and guiding them in their quests for wisdom and justice. The olive tree she donated has become an enduring symbol of the city, reminding everyone of the goddess' goodness and protection.

Fact 72 - The Healing Power of the Centaur Chiron

Chiron, the wisest and most righteous of the centaurs, was known throughout ancient Greece for his exceptional skills in medicine and healing. Son of Saturn and Philyra, he differed from the other centaurs, often brutal and savage, by his gentle and erudite nature. It was in his cave on Mount Pelion that Chiron educated and cared for heroes and gods.

Among his most famous pupils were Asclepius, the god of medicine, Achilles, and Hercules. Chiron taught them the art of healing, hunting, and other disciplines necessary for future heroes. His knowledge of medicinal plants was unmatched and he was able to heal almost any wound and disease.

Ironically, Chiron was accidentally wounded by a poisoned arrow fired by Hercules, his own student. Even with all his knowledge, he could not heal himself and finally asked Zeus to let him die to escape his eternal pain. In recognition of his wisdom and goodness, Zeus placed him among the stars in the form of a constellation.

Thus, Chiron's legacy lives on in the starry sky, reminding mortals of the wise centaur's precious teachings and unwavering dedication to the art of healing.

Fact 73 - The Lotus Flower Trap for Odysseus

In Homer's epic odyssey, Odysseus and his crew encounter a multitude of challenges and obstacles, one of the most insidious of which is the island of the Lotushagus. The Lotus Eaters were a people who lived on an exclusive diet of lotus flowers, a plant with sedative and amnesic effects. When Odysseus' companions tasted this flower, they instantly forgot their mission and their desire to return home.

The lotus had the power to plunge those who consumed it into a state of contentment and forgetfulness of cares, diverting them from their path and responsibilities. Odysseus, quickly realizing the danger, had to use all his strength and cunning to snatch his men from the flower's grip and bring them back to their ship.

This myth highlights the dangers of complacency and forgetting life goals. Odysseus, through his leadership and determination, managed to save his men from this bittersweet temptation and put them back on the road back to Ithaca.

The episode of the Lotus Eaters in the Odyssey serves as a powerful metaphor for the dangers of laziness and self-forgetfulness, emphasizing the importance of perseverance and vigilance in the pursuit of one's goals.

Fact 74 - The misadventures of Io, pursued by a horsefly

Io, a priestess of the temple of Hera in Greek mythology, had a series of extraordinary and tragic adventures due to Zeus' interest in her. To protect her from the jealousy of his wife Hera, Zeus transformed Io into a beautiful white heifer. However, Hera, not being fooled, asked for the cow as a gift and placed Argos, a hundred-eyed giant, to watch over her.

Hermes was sent by Zeus to liberate Io, and he managed to put Argos to sleep by telling him stories and playing music. After killing Argos, Io was freed, but Hera, furious, sent a horsefly to sting and harass her relentlessly. Io wandered the world, tormented and restless.

During his journey, Io crossed the Bosphorus, which takes its name from its passage ("boos" meaning cow and "poros" meaning passage). She eventually reached Egypt, where Zeus turned her back into a human. She gave birth to a son, Epaphus, and became a figure in Egyptian mythology under the name Isis.

This story, full of twists and turns, highlights the complexity of the relationship between gods and mortals in Greek mythology. It also illustrates how, even transformed and pursued, Io managed to leave an indelible imprint on the world, showing persistence in the face of adversity.

Fact 75 - The Abduction of Europa by Zeus in Bull

One of the most famous metamorphoses of Zeus, the supreme god of Olympus, is when he transforms into a white bull to kidnap Europa, a beautiful Phoenician princess. Attracted by the gentleness and beauty of the animal, Europa approached and, taken with affection, climbed onto its back. It was at this point that Zeus took the opportunity to flee with her, crossing the seas to the island of Crete.

On the island, Zeus returned to his original form and revealed his true identity to Europa. Amazed and seduced, she accepted his love, and from their union three sons were born, including Minos who was to become one of the greatest kings of Crete. The history of Europa and Zeus has given rise to many works of art throughout the ages, immortalizing this legend.

The European continent takes its name from Princess Europe, highlighting the profound impact of this story on Western culture and history. This episode perfectly illustrates how the Greek gods interacted with mortals, blending love, desire, and power in an intricate and eternal dance.

So, the next time you look at a map of Europe, remember this fascinating story and the extraordinary journey of a princess on the back of a divine bull. It's a vibrant reminder of how myths and legends can shape our world, far beyond ancient narratives.

Fact 76 - Hephaestus' Laughter That Makes Olympus Tremble

Hephaestus, the god of blacksmithing and metallurgy in Greek mythology, is often portrayed as a serious and hard-working character, but he had his moment of glory that left an indelible imprint on Olympus. He was a lame god, rejected by his mother Hera at birth because of his ugliness. Despite this, he became one of the most talented and respected gods.

One day, an argument broke out between Zeus and Hera, and none of the gods of Olympus were able to ease the tension. Hephaestus, with his ingenious wit, decided to take matters into his own hands. He created a magical throne and gave it to his mother, Hera. When she sat down, she found herself trapped, and the gods were unable to free her.

Hephaestus agreed to release her on the condition that Aphrodite, the goddess of love and beauty, be given in marriage. The gods, relieved and amused by Hephaestus' ingenious trick, burst out laughing, a laugh so loud that it made Olympus tremble. This moment of joy showed a different side of Hephaestus and left a trace of happiness and humor among the gods.

So, the next time you hear about Hephaestus, remember that he was not only the lame blacksmith, but also the one who brought laughter and joy in moments of tension on Olympus. His laugh resonates as a reminder that even the gods needed moments of relaxation and happiness.

Fact 77 - The Golden Rain, Zeus' gift to Danaë

In Greek myths, Zeus' love for mortals is a constant, and the story of Danaë is no exception. Danaë, daughter of King Acrisios of Argos, was imprisoned in a brazen tower by her father. The latter, having learned from an oracle that the son of Danaë would be the cause of his ruin, hoped thus to keep all the suitors at bay.

However, Zeus, in love with the beautiful Danaë, found an ingenious way to reach her. It turned into a shower of glittering gold and managed to seep through the gaps in the tower. In this glittering form, he united with Danaë, and from their union was born a son, Perseus, destined to be one of the greatest heroes of ancient Greece.

The story of Danaë and the Golden Rain demonstrates Zeus' perseverance in his quest for love, as well as his ability to outwit the most formidable obstacles. It also illustrates how the fates prophesied by Greek oracles tended to come true, often unexpectedly, highlighting the inevitability of fate in Greek mythology.

The myth of Danaë is thus a fascinating testament to the power of love, divine cunning and the inescapable force of fate, weaving together the central themes that run through so many Greek mythological stories. A tale that, through the ages, continues to amaze and inspire, recalling the magic and mystery that envelops the legends of ancient Greece.

Fact 78 - Ganymede's Rise to the Rank of Deity

Ganymede, the young Trojan prince of unparalleled beauty, had an extraordinary adventure that propelled him from earth to heaven. Enchanted by her beauty and grace, Zeus decided to kidnap her to make her his cupbearer, the servant who would pour nectar and ambrosia to the gods of Olympus. To accomplish this abduction, Zeus took the form of a majestic eagle and seized Ganymede in his mighty talons, carrying him away from his homeland.

Ganymede's father, King Tros, was understandably devastated by the loss of his beloved son. In compensation, Zeus sent Hermes to bring divine horses to Tros, assuring that Ganymede would henceforth live forever among the gods. Ganymede thus became the cupbearer of the gods, serving them nectar and ambrosia, and was immortalized among the stars in the form of the constellation Aquarius.

The story of Ganymede highlights the capricious nature of the Greek gods, but also illustrates their ability to offer generous compensations. Ganymede himself is a symbol of ascension and transcendence, moving from mortal to divinity, and is a reminder that even in the darkest of times, Greek mythology finds ways to infuse hope and splendor.

Fact 79 - Aphrodite's Magic Mirror

Aphrodite, the goddess of love and beauty in Greek mythology, possessed a priceless object: a magic mirror. This was no ordinary mirror; He had the unique power to reveal the true nature of anyone who dared to look at it. Through this mirror, Aphrodite could see beyond appearances and illusions, discerning inner beauty and hidden ugliness.

This mirror also served Aphrodite in her dealings with other gods and mortals. She used it to thwart malicious plans and to guide those who sought her help to a deeper awareness of themselves. Thus, the mirror was not only an instrument of vanity, but also a tool for wisdom and introspection.

Ancient stories tell how this mirror played a crucial role in some of the most memorable adventures in Greek mythology. For example, he helped Psyche, a mere mortal, realize true love and overcome obstacles to join her lover Eros.

Aphrodite's magic mirror reminds us that beauty is not always what it seems, and that a deeper understanding of ourselves and others can be revealed if we dare to look beyond the surfaces.

Fact 80 - Aurora's Tears Turning Dew

In Greek mythology, Aurora, also known as Eos in Greek, is the goddess of dawn. Every morning, she opens the gates of heaven to let the chariot of the sun travel across the sky, heralding the beginning of a new day. But behind this daily task lies a moving story of loss and grief that explains the morning dew.

Aurora was madly in love with a mortal named Tithon. She asked Zeus to grant her immortality so that they could spend eternity together. Zeus granted his request, but Aurora forgot to ask for eternal youth for Tithon. Over time, Tithon grew old and lost all his vigor, leaving Aurora with a love that could no longer be reciprocated in the same way.

Heartbroken, Aurora's tears began to fall each morning. The ancient Greeks believed that these tears turned to dew, lining the world with a blanket of glittering pearls. It was both a tribute to her lost love and a daily reminder of the ephemeral nature of beauty and youth.

So, whenever you see the morning dew, remember the story of Aurora and her immortal love, and that even in sorrow there can be beauty and an opportunity for renewal.

Fact 81 - Apples of Discord, Cause of Great Quarrels

Apples of Discord play a crucial role in Greek mythology, being at the origin of one of the most famous conflicts in ancient history: the Trojan War. These apples are not ordinary fruits, but rather objects of power and discord, carrying messages intended to sow discord. The story begins with the marriage of Peleus and Thetis, to which all the deities are invited, except for Eris, the goddess of discord.

Eris, furious at not having been invited, decides to take revenge by throwing a golden apple into the banquet hall, with the inscription "To the most beautiful". Three goddesses, Hera, Athena, and Aphrodite, claim the title and the apple, leading to a divine dispute. To decide, they turn to Paris, a mortal, instructing him to designate the most beautiful of them.

Each of the goddesses tries to bribe Paris with grandiose promises, and he ends up choosing Aphrodite, seduced by her promise to offer her the love of the most beautiful woman in the world, Helen. This choice leads directly to Helen's abduction and the outbreak of the Trojan War, proving that even a simple apple can have devastating consequences when intertwined with vanity and rivalry.

Fact 82 - Achilles' Journey to the Realm of the Dead

Achilles, the legendary hero of the Trojan War, has had a fascinating adventure that has taken him to the far reaches of the realm of the dead. Known for his unparalleled strength and bravery, he was nevertheless tormented by questions about his own destiny and the truths of existence. Searching for answers, he decided to embark on a perilous journey to consult the shadow of the soothsayer Tiresias in the afterlife.

Guided by the precise instructions of the sorceress Circe, Achilles crossed the borders between worlds, a rare and dangerous feat even for a hero of his caliber. In the darkness of the realm of the dead, he was confronted with unsettling visions, including that of his own deceased friend, Patroclus, whose encounter was filled with emotion and revelations about the ephemeral nature of life.

Achilles also had exchanges with other illustrious souls, such as Ajax and Agamemnon, exploring the depths of wisdom and knowledge. These conversations informed his understanding of life, death, and honor, central themes in his epic story.

Ultimately, Achilles' journey into the realm of the dead was a quest for truth and meaning, reflecting the values and beliefs of ancient Greece. He returned to the world of the living transformed, with a renewed perspective on his own existence and the sacrifices inherent in heroic living.

Fact 83 - Apollo's Laurel Wreath

The laurel wreath is a symbol strongly associated with Apollo, the Greek god of music, poetry, light, and divination. This association has its origins in a fascinating myth that reflects the values and beliefs of ancient Greece. Daphne, a wood nymph and daughter of the river god Peneus, caught Apollo's attention. Desperately in love, Apollo pursued her with insatiable ardour.

However, Daphne, seeking to preserve her virginity, implored her father's help to escape Apollo. Peneus granted her wish by turning her into a laurel tree, an act that both saved Daphne and broke Apollo's heart. As a tribute to his lost love and to remember Daphne forever, Apollo made the laurel tree his sacred tree and made himself a wreath out of its leaves.

This laurel wreath has become a powerful symbol of victory, glory, and immortality, worn by emperors, generals, and poets throughout history. She embodied excellence, inspiration, and spiritual elevation, key aspects of the cult of Apollo.

The story of Apollo's laurel wreath highlights the ability of Greek mythology to weave deep and symbolic narratives, connecting gods and mortals in an intricate web of love, loss, and reverence. This tradition continues to influence contemporary culture and art, a testament to the timeless power of these ancient myths.

Fact 84 - The Sweet Sleep Induced by Hypnos

Hypnos, in Greek mythology, is the god personifying sleep, and his power over mortals and immortals is both feared and admired. The twin brother of Thanatos, the personification of death, Hypnos lives in a dark palace located in the uncharted and mysterious lands, surrounded by poppies and other sleep-inducing plants. Its influence extends throughout the world, bringing rest and dreams to those who succumb to its power.

He is often depicted holding a horn filled with sleep potions, which he uses to instantly put anyone who crosses his path to sleep. Even the gods of Olympus are not immune to his influence, and there are many stories where Hypnos plays a key role in appeasing the deities with his restful sleep.

One of the most famous stories involves Hypnos helping Hera deceive Zeus, putting the king of the gods to sleep so that Hera could manipulate the Trojan War in favor of the Greeks. Although Zeus was furious when he discovered the deception, he could not deny the effectiveness of Hypnos' power.

The legacy of Hypnos lives on in contemporary culture, with its name being the origin of the word "hypnosis", a practice aimed at inducing a state of concentration and deep relaxation. Thus, the god of sleep continues to influence our lives, reminding us of the importance of rest and dreams in human well-being.

Fact 85 - The Power of the Muses on Inspiration

The Muses, in Greek mythology, are nine goddesses daughters of Zeus and Mnemosyne, the goddess of memory. They embody the arts and sciences, and are considered the source of inspiration for artists, writers, and scientists. Each of the Muses is associated with a specific field of arts and sciences, ranging from epic poetry and music to history and astronomy.

Their influence is vast and powerful, guiding creators through their dreams and thoughts. The ancient Greeks believed that the Muses visited artists and scholars, whispering ideas to them and helping them solve complex problems. This belief emphasizes the importance of inspiration and creativity in ancient Greek society.

The Muses were also worshipped through festivals and art competitions, where participants invoked their help to excel in their art. The winners of these competitions were often considered to have received direct favor from the Muses.

Today, the legacy of the Muses lives on, with their name used to describe a source of inspiration. They serve as a reminder of the connection between creativity, knowledge and divinity, and continue to inspire those who seek to push the boundaries of art and science.

Fact 86 - The Sacred Fire Guarded by the Vestal Virgins

In the heart of ancient Rome, the Vestal Virgins, priestesses of the goddess Vesta, held a crucial responsibility: to keep the sacred fire burning in the Temple of Vesta. This rite was of paramount importance, as it symbolized the perpetuity and stability of the city. According to Roman belief, if the fire was extinguished, it portended disasters for Rome and its people.

Vestal Virgins were chosen at a very young age, often before the age of ten, and were destined for thirty years of service. During this period, they had to remain virgins and entirely dedicated to their task. Their role was not limited to monitoring the fire; they also participated in various religious rites and ceremonies, playing an essential role in the religious life of Rome.

The punishment for failing in their duties was severe. If the fire was extinguished, the responsible Vestal Virgin, was punished, and if she broke her vow of chastity, she was buried alive. These strict rules emphasize the importance given to their role in Roman society.

The institution of the Vestal Virgins lasted for nearly a thousand years, testifying to the importance of the sacred and tradition in ancient Rome. Their dedication and integrity continue to be admired, and the story of the Vestal Virgins remains a poignant example of the connection between religion and state in antiquity.

Fact 87 - The Birth of Dionysus from a Thigh of Zeus

Greek mythology is full of extraordinary stories, and the birth of Dionysus, god of wine, is no exception. The son of Zeus and the mortal Semele, Dionysus had a tumultuous start to his life, to say the least. Semele, seduced by Zeus, is deceived by Hera, Zeus' wife, and asks to see her lover in all his divine splendor. Unable to resist such a sight, Semele perishes, leaving her unborn child in a perilous situation.

It is then that Zeus intervenes, taking the unfinished child and sewing it into his own thigh, where Dionysus completes his development. This extraordinary method of birth endows Dionysus with both a divine and mortal nature, a recurring theme in his mythology and worship.

As an adult, Dionysus became a central figure in the Greek pantheon, associated with the vine, wine and celebration, but also with transformations and excesses. His cult is characterized by its ecstatic mysteries and rites, often accompanied by wine and frenzied dancing.

Thus, the singular birth of Dionysus symbolizes not only his duality between the divine and mortal worlds, but also the liberating and chaotic aspect of his nature, which continues to fascinate and intrigue mythology lovers to this day.

Fact 88 - The Dance of the Stars, Girls of Atlas

In the vast starry sky of Greek mythology, the Pleiades hold a special place. These seven sisters, daughters of the titan Atlas, have been immortalized in the constellations, creating a mesmerizing celestial spectacle. According to legend, the Pleiades were so beautiful and graceful that Zeus placed them in the sky to protect them from the relentless advances of Orion, the hunter.

Their celestial dance is breathtakingly beautiful, visible to the naked eye in the night sky. The Pleiades, also known as the Seven Sisters, are a cluster of stars in the constellation Taurus. Although they are said to be seven, only six stars are usually visible, adding a layer of mystery to their story.

According to mythology, the seventh sister, Merope, hid in shame after marrying a mortal. This story emphasizes the importance of divinity and purity in ancient Greek culture.

By inviting you to look up at the sky, you can contemplate the eternal dance of the Pleiades, a living legacy of Greek mythology, mixing beauty, mystery and the eternal intrigues of the gods.

Fact 89 - The Sun's Course, Drawn by Helios

Every day, a grandiose spectacle unfolds in the sky of Greek mythology, orchestrated by the god Helios. Driving his chariot drawn by four flamboyant horses, he makes a celestial crossing, marking the eternal cycle of day and night. Its course begins at dawn in the east and ends at dusk in the west in a display of divine power and perseverance.

Helios is often confused with Apollo, another god associated with the sun. However, in ancient Greek mythology, Helios is specifically the sun god, a daily witness to the actions of mortals and immortals. His piercing vision leaves no stone unturned, making him a symbol of truth and clarity.

Legend has it that one day, his son Phaethon begged to drive the solar chariot. Helios, in a moment of paternal weakness, agreed. Unfortunately, Phaethon lost control, endangering Earth and the sky, until Zeus intervened to stop the catastrophe.

Thus, Helios' daily run is more than just a journey across the sky; It is a reminder of cosmic order, divine vigilance, and the consequences of human desire for power and recognition.

Fact 90 - The Story of Cephalus and the Dawn

The story of Cephalus, a mortal hunter of exceptional beauty, and the aurora, the goddess Eos, is a tale of passion and melancholy. Eos, madly in love with Cephalus, kidnapped her and took her with her. Despite the divine favors and immortality offered to him, Cephalus could not forget his wife Procris, whom he had left behind.

Heartbroken by the separation, Cephalus implored Eos to let him return to Procris. Touched by his sincere love, Eos agreed, but she feared that he would not be faithful. So she sowed doubt in his mind, making him fear that Procris would be unfaithful to her. This doubt poisoned Cephalus' heart, and she decided to test his wife's faithfulness.

The tragically ill-conceived test led to Procris' death, leaving Cephalus overwhelmed with remorse and pain. The dawn, in its sadness, turned Cephalus into a star, perpetuating his story in the night sky.

Thus, the story of Cephalus and the dawn is a poignant reminder of the consequences of doubt and jealousy, even in the face of true and sincere love.

Fact 91 - The Adventures of Odysseus and the Sirens

Mermaids, mythological creatures with haunting voices, played a crucial role in Homer's legendary epic Odyssey. Odysseus, the cunning king of Ithaca, had been warned by Circe of the irresistible temptation of the siren song. He was fascinated and determined to hear their melody without succumbing to their deadly charm.

To protect himself and his crew, Odysseus took shrewd measures. He had his sailors' ears plugged with beeswax and ordered it to be tied to the mast of his ship. Thus prepared, he made sure that only he could hear the sirens' song, while his crew would be safe from their seduction.

As the ship approached the sirens, their melodious song filled the air. Odysseus, captivated, begged to be released, but his sailors, faithful to his orders, kept him securely bound until they were out of range. His life was spared by his own foresight.

Odysseus thus demonstrated that intelligence and prudence can triumph over temptation and danger, a timeless and universal message from one of the most famous stories in Greek mythology.

Fact 92 - The Beauty of Adonis Who Seduces Two Goddesses

Adonis, famous for her dazzling beauty, captivated the hearts of two powerful goddesses of Olympus: Aphrodite, the goddess of love and beauty, and Persephone, the queen of the Underworld. Born from the singular union of Myrrha and his own father, Adonis inherited such exceptional beauty that she immediately caught Aphrodite's attention.

The goddess of love, madly in love, hid Adonis in a casket that she entrusted to Persephone to protect him. However, Persephone was also seduced by his beauty and refused to return him to Aphrodite. The dispute between the two goddesses was so intense that it required the intervention of Zeus, the king of the gods.

Zeus, in his wisdom, settled the dispute by deciding that Adonis would spend one-third of the year with each of the goddesses and the remaining third wherever he pleased. Adonis chooses to spend his free time with Aphrodite, showing his preference for the goddess of love.

This story illustrates not only the irresistible power of beauty in Greek mythology, but also how the gods themselves could be enamored with mortals, emphasizing the universal themes of love, jealousy, and desire.

Fact 93 - The Snake Charmer Asclepius

Asclepius, the god of medicine in Greek mythology, was renowned for his extraordinary healing skills and for his unique association with snakes. Son of Apollo, the god of healing and music, and Coronis, a mortal, Asclepius inherited his father's gifts and pushed them to unparalleled levels. He learned the art of medicine under the tutelage of the centaur Chiron, who taught him how to use plants and herbs to cure diseases.

The snake, a symbol of rebirth and healing due to its ability to molt its skin, became the emblem of Asclepius. According to legend, he observed a snake using herbs to resurrect another snake, which revealed to him the secrets of life and death. This discovery allowed him to resurrect the dead, a power that eventually caught the attention of Zeus.

Zeus, worried that Asclepius' power might upset the balance between life and death, decided to strike him with a bolt of lightning. However, in recognition of his contributions to medicine, Zeus placed him among the stars in the form of the constellation Serpentarius.

To this day, the Staff of Asclepius, a snake coiled around a stem, remains a universal symbol of medicine, a testament to the lasting impact of the snake charmer of Greek mythology on our world.

Fact 94 - The Exploits of the Hero Bellerophon

Bellerophon, one of the most fascinating heroes of Greek mythology, is famous for his daring exploits and tragic fate. Son of Glaucos and grandson of Sisyphus, he gained eternal fame by taming Pegasus, the winged horse, thanks to a magical harness given to him by Athena. On the back of Pegasus, Bellerophon performed many feats, the most famous of which is the defeat of the Chimera, a terrifying creature that is half lion, half goat, with a snake's tail.

Bellerophon's fame quickly climbed, attracting the attention of gods and mortals alike. Proitos, the king of Tiryns, jealous of his popularity and influenced by malicious rumors, sent Bellerophon to confront the Chimera, hoping for his death. However, the hero, guided by divine signs, managed to defeat the beast, proving his valor and courage.

After his victories, Bellerophon met an unfortunate fate. Attempting to reach Olympus on the back of Pegasus, he was hurled to earth by a gadfly sent by Zeus, punished for his pride. Bellerophon ended his days wandering, blinded and broken, a poignant reminder of the fine line between heroism and hubris in Greek mythology.

Thus, Bellerophon's story remains a captivating tale of glory and fall, illustrating heroic greatness and the perils of pride in the ancient world.

Fact 95 - The Eternal Wisdom of Athena's Owl

The owl, a symbol of wisdom and knowledge, is closely associated with Athena, the Greek goddess of wisdom and war. This nocturnal bird became a powerful emblem in Greek mythology, reflecting the values and attributes of the goddess herself. You may have seen depictions of Athena with an owl resting on her shoulder, symbolizing her intimate connection with wisdom and intelligence.

The presence of the owl in Greek iconography is no coincidence. The ancient Greeks believed that the owl had the ability to see through darkness, thus representing insight and the ability to discern truth. It was a valuable guide for mortals and gods alike, illuminating the path to knowledge and understanding.

The city of Athens, named in honor of the goddess Athena, adopted the owl as its symbol. Coins minted in Athens often bore the image of the owl, emphasizing the importance of wisdom and intelligence in Athenian society. This association between the owl, Athena, and the city of Athens has become one of the most enduring symbols of ancient Greece.

Even today, Athena's owl is a powerful symbol of wisdom and intelligence, recalling the cultural and philosophical heritage of ancient Greece.

Fact 96 - The Tragic Love of Eros and Psyche

Eros, the god of love, falls madly in love with Psyche, a mortal whose beauty is so dazzling that she even arouses the jealousy of Aphrodite, the goddess of love and beauty. Yet, their love must overcome many trials, instigated by a resentful Aphrodite.

Eros, acting in secret, becomes Psyche's lover, but he imposes one condition on her: she must never try to see his face. However, driven by curiosity and doubts sown by her envious sisters, Psyche breaks this prohibition and lights up Eros' face as he sleeps. Awakened and hurt by his betrayal, Eros leaves her immediately, plunging Psyche into deep despair.

Determined to win back the lost love, Psyche implores Aphrodite to give her a chance to prove her love. The goddess, seizing the opportunity to torment her, subjects Psyche to a series of seemingly insurmountable trials. However, with the help of various deities and her own determination, Psyche overcomes every obstacle, proving her unwavering love for Eros.

Eventually, touched by her perseverance and true love, Zeus himself intervenes, granting immortality to Psyche so that she can be reunited with Eros. Their love, once hampered by the whims of the gods, becomes eternal, symbolizing the victory of true love over obstacles and trials.

Fact 97 - The Island of the Lotus Eaters

The island of the Lotus Eaters is a mysterious place in Greek mythology, evoked in Homer's Odyssey, during Odysseus' long journey home after the Trojan War. This island is inhabited by the Lotus Eaters, a people who feed exclusively on the fruits of the lotus, a plant with amazing and potentially dangerous properties. Odysseus and his companions, exhausted by their journey, stop there, unaware of the surprises that this land has in store.

By accepting the hospitality of the Lotus, some of Odysseus' companions taste the fruits of the lotus. Soon, they fall under the spell of this bewitching fruit, losing all desire to return to their homeland, Ithaca. The lotus has the power to make the one who consumes it forget his responsibilities and his past, plunging him into a state of bliss and carefreeness.

Odysseus, realizing the danger, acts quickly and decisively. He orders his men to forcibly drag the seduced companions away from Lotus Isle, saving them from oblivion and loss. This story, full of adventure and lessons, emphasizes the importance of resilience and a sense of duty, even in the face of the sweetest and most intoxicating temptations.

The episode of the island of the Lotus Eaters remains a striking example of the many challenges and seductions that Odysseus and his men encounter during their odyssey.

Fact 98 - Niobe's Weeping Becomes an Eternal Source

In Greek mythology, the story of Niobe is synonymous with grief and loss, turning his name into an eternal symbol of mourning. Niobe, daughter of Tantalus and wife of Amphion, was a queen endowed with great pride, who had the audacity to compare herself to the goddess Leto, claiming to be a better mother because she had had more children. Offended by this arrogance, Leto sent his children, Apollo and Artemis, to punish Niobe.

Apollo and Artemis, armed with their bows, slew all the children of Niobe, one after the other, before his eyes. Inconsolable, Niobe wept incessantly until the gods, moved by her pain, turned her to stone. But even when transformed into a statue, Niobe's tears never ceased to flow, forming a spring that never dries up.

Today, this story is a poignant reminder of the importance of humility and the dangers of proud comparison with the divine. It also teaches compassion, showing that even the gods can be touched by human suffering, to the point of granting it a form of eternity.

As you delve into this story, you discover one of the many ways in which Greek mythology explores the universal themes of loss, mourning, and redemption. Niobe, through her ordeal, becomes an inexhaustible source of inspiration, reminding everyone of the strength that can be born from the deepest despair.

Fact 99 - Theseus' Victory over Procrustes

The adventure of Theseus, the Athenian hero, with Procrustes is one of the most gripping stories in Greek mythology. Procrustes, a brigand living in the mountains of Attica, had a particularly cruel method of entertaining his guests. He forced them to lie down on an iron bed, adjusting their size to that of the bed by barbarous means: he stretched those that were too short and cut off the limbs of those that were too long.

Theseus, on his way to Athens, met Procrustes and was subjected to this brutal ordeal. However, the young hero, cunning and strong, turned Procrustes' cruel fate against himself. He overpowered the brigand and laid him on his own torture bed, subjecting him to the same fate reserved for his victims.

This victory of Theseus symbolizes the triumph of justice over cruelty and cunning over brute force. It also demonstrates the hero's ability to turn desperate situations in his favor, a recurring theme in the heroic tales of ancient Greece.

The legend of Theseus and Procrustes continues to be a powerful reminder of perseverance and ingenuity, inspiring everyone to never underestimate their own inner strength in the face of adversity. The Athenian hero remains a model of cunning and courage, perfectly exemplifying how triumph over cruelty and injustice is not only possible, but essential.

Fact 100 - The Morning Star, Symbol of Hope

In the rich tapestry of Greek mythology, the morning star occupies a prominent place, embodying hope and rebirth. Known as Phosphorus, this celestial phenomenon is none other than the planet Venus, visible at dawn, announcing the imminent arrival of the day. This star has always been associated with notions of hope and new beginnings, a light guiding travelers and lost souls through the darkness.

Myth has it that Phosphorus is the son of Dawn, the goddess who brings daylight. Its presence in the morning sky is a constant reminder that even after the darkest night, the day is about to rise. It is a powerful symbol of optimism and perseverance, inspiring everyone to remain hopeful even in the most difficult times.

In literature and art, the morning star has often been depicted as a guide, a messenger of good news and positive change. It inspires poets, artists, and all those who seek light in the darkness, reminding them that the new day brings new opportunities and a chance to start over.

Thus, Phosphorus, the morning star, remains a powerful emblem of hope and renewal in Greek culture and mythology. It is a constant invitation to look forward, to believe in the possibility of a better future and to never give up, no matter the circumstances.

Conclusion

There you have it, dear reader, the journey through the fascinating depths of Greek mythology is coming to an end. A hundred stories, a hundred moments of pure wonder, and as many opportunities to learn and be amazed. We hope that these pages have allowed you to dive into the depths of the Greek imagination, and that you take with you stories full of wisdom, bravery, and love.

Every fact, every anecdote, has been carefully chosen and narrated to transport you to a world where the gods walk among men, and where the extraordinary mingles with the everyday. Perhaps you have found inspiration in the heroic exploits of Perseus or Athena, or perhaps you have felt pain and joy in the tragedies and loves of the gods.

Greek mythology, although ancient, remains timeless and universal. Her stories speak to themes that still resonate today: love, loss, ambition, revenge, and the search for meaning. She reminds us of our humanity, with its flaws and greatness, and continues to inspire artists, writers, and dreamers around the world.

Greek mythology is a treasure waiting to be explored, and each story is a gateway to a world of adventure and discovery. See you soon for new explorations into the myths and legends of the world!

Marc Dresgui

Quiz

1) What is the fruit that, according to Greek mythology, makes people forgetful of their homes?

    a) Apple
    b) Fishing
    c) Lotophagi
    d) Grenada

2) In Greek mythology, which river is associated with forgetfulness?

    a) Styx
    b) Lethe
    c) Acheron
    d) Peneus

3) What is the name of the winged horse that Bellerophon tamed?

    a) Arion
    b) Xanthos
    c) Pegasus
    d) Bucephalus

4) What is the fruit associated with the Garden of the Hesperides?

    a) Golden apples

b) Silver pears
c) Crystal plums
d) Diamond cherries

5) Who is Achilles' mother?

a) Hera
b) Thetis
c) Athena
d) Aphrodite

6) What is special about the island of Aeolus?

a) It floats in the air
b) It's invisible
c) It's constantly on the move
d) It is guarded by giants

7) What is Cassandra's unique gift?

a) Superhuman Strength
b) The Prophecy
c) Healing
d) Metamorphosis

8) What is the work assigned to the Danaids after their death?

a) Endless Weaving

b) Filling a bottomless barrel
c) Pushing a Rock Forever
d) Cooking for the Gods

9) **What animal is associated with Dionysus?**
   a) The Lion
   b) The Bull
   c) The Horse
   d) The Panther

10) **What is Athena's sacred tree?**
    a) The Apple Tree
    b) The Olive Tree
    c) The Fig Tree
    d) Oak

11) **What gift did Daedalus give to Ariadne to help Theseus?**
    a) A Sword
    b) A shield
    c) A Golden Thread
    d) A lamp

12) **How did Heracles manage to clean the Augean stables in a single day?**

   a) Stopping time
   b) Using fire
   c) By diverting two rivers
   d) Asking the gods for help

13) **What is the item that Perseus uses to defeat Medusa?**

   a) A shield
   b) A mirror
   c) A Sword
   d) A Polished Shield

14) **What is Helios' means of transport across the sky?**

   a) A horse-drawn chariot
   b) A boat
   c) A magic carpet
   d) A hot air balloon

15) **What plant allows Odysseus to resist the influence of sirens?**

   a) Ambrosia
   b) The Lotus
   c) Laurel

d) The moly

16) Who is the goddess who transforms into a doe to escape a suitor?

   a) Artemis
   b) Aphrodite
   c) Hera
   d) Britomartis

17) What bird is associated with Zeus as a messenger?

   a) The Dove
   b) The Raven
   c) The Eagle
   d) The Owl

18) Who among the following is the goddess of the hunt?

   a) Demeter
   b) Hestia
   c) Artemis
   d) Hera

19) How did Theseus kill Procrustes?

   a) By crushing it under a rock
   b) By cutting it with his own axe

c) By poisoning it
d) Drowning it

20) What is the symbol associated with Athena and wisdom?

a) The Lion
b) The Owl
c) The Horse
d) The Bull

Answers

1) What is the fruit that, according to Greek mythology, makes people forgetful of their homes?

Correct answer: c)Lotophagi

2) In Greek mythology, which river is associated with forgetfulness?

Correct answer: b)Lethe

3) What is the name of the winged horse that Bellerophon tamed?

Correct answer: c)Pegasus

4) What is the fruit associated with the Garden of the Hesperides?

Correct answer: a)Golden apples

5) Who is Achilles' mother?

Correct answer: b)Thetis

6) What is special about the island of Aeolus?

Correct answer: d) It is guarded by giants

7) What is Cassandra's unique gift?

Correct answer: b) Prophecy

8) What is the work assigned to the Danaids after their death?

Correct answer: b) Filling a bottomless barrel

9) What animal is associated with Dionysus?

Correct answer: d) The panther

10) What is Athena's sacred tree?

Correct answer: b) The olive tree

11) What gift did Daedalus give to Ariadne to help Theseus?

Correct answer: c) A golden thread

12) How did Heracles manage to clean the Augean stables in a single day?

Correct answer: c) By diverting two rivers

13) What is the item that Perseus uses to defeat Medusa?

Correct answer: d) A polished shield

14) What is Helios' means of transport across the sky?

Correct answer: a) A horse-drawn chariot

15) What plant allows Odysseus to resist the influence of sirens?

Correct answer: d) Moly

16) Who is the goddess who transforms into a doe to escape a suitor?

Correct answer: d) Britomartis

17) What bird is associated with Zeus as a messenger?

Correct answer: c) The eagle

18) Who among the following is the goddess of the hunt?

Correct answer: c)Artemis

19) How did Theseus kill Procrustes?

Correct answer: b) Cutting it with your own axe

20) What is the symbol associated with Athena and wisdom?

Correct answer: b) The owl

Printed in Great Britain
by Amazon